Bill Huebsch

Whole
Community
Catechesis

in plain english

TWENTY-THIRD PUBLICATIONS
185 WILLOW STREET • PO BOX 180 • MYSTIC, CT 06355
TEL: 1-800-321-0411 • FAX: 1-800-572-0788
E-MAIL: ttpubs@aol.com • www.twentythirdpublications.com

Definitions based on entries in *The American Heritage Dictionary of the English Language*, third edition. (New York: Houghton Mifflin Company, 1996)

Third printing 2003

Twenty-Third Publications
A Division of Bayard
185 Willow Street
P.O. Box 180
Mystic, CT 06355
(860) 536-2611 or (800) 321-0411
www.twentythirdpublications.com

ISBN:1-58595-184-6
Library of Congress Catalog Card Number: 2001135980
Printed in the U.S.A.

Dedication

To Bishop Raymond Lucker

"What I came to see during the Second Vatican Council is that revelation involved God's self-communication to us. God communicated the inner mysteries of God to us. And we can never...adequately explain or express the revelation of God."

—Bishop Ray Lucker
The National Catholic Reporter, May 25, 2001

Contents

Introduction

Section 1: The New Framework

Section 2: Nuts & Bolts

Appendices

Introduction

Where does the idea for whole community catechesis come from?

Whole community catechesis is drawn from (1) careful consideration of the way Jesus taught, along with (2) reflections on the teachings of Vatican II, (3) the wonderful direction provided by the GDC itself, and (4) the emerging consensus in the catechetical community that the present "schoolhouse" framework within which catechesis is provided lacks some essential elements.

The name, whole community catechesis or total parish catechesis or faith formation for all (every parish seems to have its own name for this), is drawn from article #254 of the GDC where it says that:

> The Christian community is the origin, locus, and goal of catechesis. Proclamation of the Gospel always begins with the Christian community and invites [people] to conversion and the following of Christ. It

The General Directory for Catechesis, usually called the GDC for short, is a guide for those who work in the ministry of catechesis. Signed by Pope John Paul II in 1997 and sent to all corners of the Catholic world, it was written in response to a directive of the Second Vatican Council which decreed that a "directory for the catechetical instruction of the Christian people" be drawn up (article 44 of the Decree on Bishops). The GDC is the international Catholic guide for catechesis.

is the same community that welcomes those who wish to know the Lord better and permeate themselves with a new life. The Christian community accompanies catechumens and those being catechized, and with maternal solicitude makes them participate in her own experience of the faith and incorporates them into herself.

The "places" where catechesis occurs, the GDC goes on to tell us, include the family, the baptismal catechumenate, the parish, Catholic schools, associations, movements, and groups of the faithful, and basic ecclesial communities.

So it's the community, the whole community, in which catechesis or faith-sharing must occur. It includes the parish ("a fraternal and welcoming family") and transcends it. And it's mainly an adult matter, but also includes children and adolescents. The GDC puts it bluntly:

Adult catechesis must be given priority. (Article 258)

Finally, again, the GDC is so clear on its insistence that catechesis is the work of the whole community. For those working in the catechetical ministries of the church this is a huge relief—but almost unbelievable. For so long, they have labored to provide religious education programs for our parishes, as though the responsibility for this was all theirs! These folks have always known in their hearts that the wider community must play a role, but now everyone is saying that. Here's what the GDC says:

In giving attention to the individual, it should not be overlooked that the recipient of catechesis is the whole Christian community and every person in it. (Article 168)

Many workers in the vineyard

Writing in 1995, Françoise Darcy-Berube laid the ground on which a new framework within which to approach catechesis could be built. In *Religious Education at a Crossroads*, she asked this question:

How can we provide a diversified, flexible, and ongoing support system for the development of a quality Christian life in the young of our communities, in their families, and in the adult population?

There will be three main ingredients in doing this, she went on to write:

> 1) A truly personalized educational care for each child and adolescent through a variety of small groups concerned with catechesis, spiritual life, and apprenticeship in Christian life.
>
> 2) A much closer, personalized, diversified, and lasting cooperation with the families of these youngsters.
>
> 3) A more efficient support network made up of meaningful, personal, inter-generational relationships and of a variety of small intentional communities within the larger community. (from pages 20-21)

Françoise Darcy-Berube is not alone in calling for a new framework within which to provide catechesis in the church, and she is not alone in believing that the new approach must be more intergenerational, more adapted to the whole community, more trusting of the households of the parish, and more focused on adults.

Dick Reichert wrote about this in NCCL's *Update* in April, 1994: "The real challenge contained in the pursuit of alternative models is to create a radical new paradigm of catechesis. It cannot simply be a process of going back to the past or making surface modifications of the present models."

Others, like Jane Regan of Boston College, have been involved in actual parish settings with models for this new approach that really work! (See the note on her book in the reading list.) "Imagining an alternative vision of catechesis, one in which the adult community is invited into the process of transformation, is the first step that needs to be taken as we move into the next millennium" (Jane Regan, "Catechesis for the Next Millennium: Focus on Adults" in *Listening*, Winter, 1998).

Likewise, Barbara West of St. Stephen's Parish in Anoka, Minnesota, has been saying for many years that the new approach to catechesis must emerge from the Sunday assembly. She knew this from her own experience in the catechumenate there. Breaking open the word each weekend was the moment of conversion for nearly every participant. Why not let the wider parish in on this secret? Working with Timothy

Mullner and the team at that parish, they piloted an entirely new framework for providing community-wide catechesis while also focusing on the needs of the youngsters in the parish and school.

Maria Harris, Gabe Moran, Tom Groome, Peter Phan, Kate Dooley OP, John Westerhoff, John Roberto, Berard Marthaler OFM, Maureen Shaughnessy SC, and countless others (this list leaves many unmentioned) are all pointing to the need for new language, models, structures, and goals. For example, John Roberto and his team have developed complete intergenerational programs at the Center for Ministry Development.

The Catechesis of the Good Shepherd provides yet another option. Parishes across the nation are experimenting and succeeding in the shift to a new, more whole community approach to providing religious education.

Just the list of those who contributed to the recent *Leader's Guide* for the U.S. bishops' pastoral letter, *Our Hearts Were Burning Within Us*, published by the USCCB, gives an impression of the breadth and depth of the movement to shift from a children's-only program of catechesis to one that embraces the whole community. Jack McBride of Madison was the general editor. Jim Kemma of Jefferson City, John Meyer of Phoenix, Margaret Ralph of Lexington, David Riley of Cincinnati, Janet Schaeffler OP of Detroit, and Diane Smith of Stockton were senior consultants. Pilots were run on the use of this guide by Ed Gordon and Gloria Reinhardt of Wilmington, Cathy Minkiewicz of Boston, and Carolyn Saucier of Jefferson City, among others.

The adult education community, folks like Ed Gordon of the Diocese of Wilmington, and Joanne Chafe of the Canadian Bishops' Conference, have been assisting the church in developing these models. The many dedicated leaders who serve on NACARE, the U.S. bishops' advisory committee on adult formation, have been calling for this shift in focus from children's-only programs to more inclusive, parish-wide ones.

In conversation with other leaders around the country, this need is obvious. Edith Prendergast RSM, who directs religious education in the Archdiocese of Los Angeles, is searching for ways to make adult formation more a norm there, for example. One of her staff people, Steven Ellair, studied intergenerational models as part of his work in the NCEA Catechetical Scholars Project. Brian Lemoi, who directs religious education in St. Petersburg, represents many others when he says that such a new approach is the future of catechesis.

Likewise, Rose Monique Peña OP, who directs religious education in the Archdiocese of Miami, sees the need for a more fully integrated adult element in all catechesis and on a bilingual basis. Like others, she is developing ideas and models in order to move in that direction. So are many, many other parish and diocesan leaders around the American church and around the world.

Mark Nuehring in the Diocese of Winona has been calling for a complete review of how catechesis is provided there. Like many others and the *General Directory for Catechesis*, he knows that adult catechesis must become the norm. Like him, Brother Ed Kiefer in New Orleans sees the need and wants to move forward with a more whole community approach. Sr. Linda Gaupin in the Diocese of Orlando, working with J. Glenn Murray SJ and others, is even now developing an approach to sacramental preparation that does this very thing: renews the whole parish in the process.

Leaders from across the spectrum and around the country are aware that this need exists. This list of folks is deficient in that so many are left off of it! Indeed, today it's hard to find a diocesan or parish director of religious education, or the head of a school religion department, who does not see this need.

También en Español. And the need for a new approach to catechesis isn't only an English language need. In fact, many other cultures who now influence the American church bring with them a much more "whole community spirit," especially in the Asian and Hispanic communities. This shift to a new catechesis is bi- and trilingual in nature!

A personal reflection on this

I'm personally enthusiastic about this approach because it seems to embrace so much of the spirit and vision of Vatican II. It's highly participatory. It relies on the domestic church and on a deep partnership between ordained and lay ministries. It is in the spirit of *aggiornamento* because it brings religious education "up to date" once again!

It retains the ancient deposit of faith but expresses it in plain, contemporary terms. It embraces the Sunday assembly for Mass as the font of catechesis, the font of parish life.

What will this new approach (for which many leaders seem to be calling!) look like? For starters, I doubt we will see one model or one program style emerge. I hope we will see bold experimentation in parish after parish. I hope we will see many ways of doing this, in fact, a different way for each parish community.

The purpose of this book is to give voice to this movement for reform and make it available to a very wide audience by describing it in good, old, plain English.

We begin in chapter one by exploring the present framework within which catechesis is provided. We called this, for lack of a better term, the "schoolhouse" framework because it's modeled so closely on how we operate our general curriculum school programs in America.

Then in chapter two we go on to give a general overview of the new framework that is emerging under the name of whole community catechesis. In chapter three we start looking at some of the nuts and bolts of the new framework called whole community catechesis. The rest of the book and the appendices all deal with nuts and bolts.

This is dangerous business precisely because the thinking and new framework associated with whole community catechesis is still emerging. As you can see from the section above, there are many contributors to this, including you as you read this and implement the parts that fit your parish and then share that with others. It's a nation-wide conversation guided, it seems, only by the Holy Spirit. But even though it's only now emerging, it's good to give voice to our early experiments and thoughts. It's good to share them as widely as possible in order to help this great renewal move forward among us.

Bill Huebsch
Pine City, Minnesota
BHuebsch@pinenet.com

The Flock

Because I'm committed to having some fun while we do this important work of renewal—and because humor is such a great avenue for both healing and happiness—I've collaborated with a great cartoonist, Jean Denton. Her work will appear at certain points throughout this manual to help us see the lighter side of this and remember that, in the end, it is the Good News that we are announcing! I hope you enjoy her work as much as I do.

SECTION 1

The New Framework

1

The "Schoolhouse" Framework

In most, but not all, parishes in America...

In the present American Catholic community, religious education in most parishes is provided within the "schoolhouse" framework. In this framework, *children* are enrolled in an optional program of *religious education* which follows the *school year* in schedules, formats, and holidays. In many places the families pay tuition for this program. The children meet in *classrooms*. In fact, in places where there is no Catholic school, parishes often prepare makeshift classroom spaces to resemble schoolrooms. The children are called *students* and their leaders are called, often, *teachers*. The term "CCD teacher" is still common, despite efforts to change it to "catechist." The students use *textbooks* that resemble schoolhouse textbooks, and the teaching method consists mainly in presenting what is found in those textbooks. *Parents* are noticeably absent, just as in general curriculum schooling. The work is done by parish catechists.

Most importantly, after about eighth grade or so, or after celebrating the sacrament of confirmation, the children believe that they have *graduated* from religious education. This sense of having graduated or finished is very strong. As a result, most post-confirmation or post-middle school religious education programs are mainly youth activity programs of one kind or another. Adult education is left undone, for the most part, because most adults in the church believe they have completed their religious education, which is, after all, for kids.

Anything that doesn't fit into this framework seems unfeasible. For example, a few years ago, when the leaders in the movement to restore the catechumenate suggested a year-round schedule for the process of formation for candidates and catechumens, the main objection in practice was that it would have to run over the summer, which is outside the school year.

In another example, many parishes have made fine attempts to provide adult education for their members. But these attempts have mainly been undertaken within the schoolhouse framework, consisting of a classroom setting, a presenter or teacher, a sense of being a student, and often even a textbook. Even parish retreats or missions usually occur within this framework.

The schoolhouse framework within which we provide religious education is common and pervasive.

And, indeed, there is a need for outright religious education for Christians to mature in their faith. Understanding the Sacred Scriptures, the church's liturgies, its history, devotions, and doctrines, is essential. This is true for Christians of all age groups. Our present schoolhouse framework does provide a structure within which this outright religious education happens very well. The textbooks are complete and beautiful. The students do seem to come away with a pretty good working knowledge of the church.

But it isn't enough.

What's not working in the schoolhouse framework?
Catechesis and liturgy are not linked

First and foremost, what's missing is the essential link between catechesis and the Sunday assembly for Mass. The liturgy is the font of the whole Christian life, including the sharing of one's faith, which is catechesis. Whole community catechesis fills in this huge gap in the present framework, as we shall see shortly.

This lack of connection between liturgy and catechesis results from something wider than the present schoolhouse framework within which religious education is provided. It stems from a misunderstanding about the hierarchy of ministries within the parish community. In many parishes it is thought that all parish programs are equally vital to community life. This results in a flat organizational chart on which liturgy is seen to be on a par with catechesis and pastoral care. (The ministry of working for justice and peace often does not even appear on this chart.)

But in fact, there is a hierarchy of ministries within the parish. The organizational chart is actually not flat. It sounds unfaithful to my colleagues in catechesis to say this, but the source and summit of the Christian life is the liturgy, not anything else. I don't know how you could read chapter one of the *Constitution on the Sacred Liturgy* from Vatican II and reach any other conclusion. Article ten is explicit in making this very point.

In the American church, where we are fascinated with organizational structures and programs, we tend to separate "departments" within our parishes. But ministry is a seamless garment. Flowing from what happens in the Sunday assembly, the various parish ministries would benefit from less departmentalization and more inter-disciplinary planning and implementation among them.

Restoring the vital and essential connection between liturgy and catechesis would help greatly in announcing the reign of God in today's world. One outcome of this might be that catechesis will become less dependent on seasonal schedules. At the moment in most parishes, catechetical ministries are closed down during parts of the major liturgical seasons of the year. Catechetical staffs tend to follow the vacation schedule of the general curriculum schools, which means they are off during the feast of Christmas and most of the Christmas season, during the Easter holidays, and if Pentecost occurs anytime after the middle of May, during that season, too.

Participation of the whole community is lacking

Second, in the schoolhouse framework the participation of the whole community is very often lacking. This produces two results.

First, the households of the parish are not involved enough in most parishes. By this, I don't mean merely that parents are not present when their children are formed in the faith. I mean, much more radically, that households are not being formed as Christian homes. Regardless of their age, members of every household have their most profound formation right in the living rooms, kitchens, and bedrooms of their home. Whole community catechesis fills in this gap, as we shall see presently.

Second, faith-sharing (which is "natural" catechesis and a rich avenue toward ongoing conversion) is not being done very often, even at the parish level itself. People gather at the parish for a variety of purposes, sometimes including catechesis, but often do not really share their faith. And yet, the principle given in the GDC is this: conversion, the turning of one's heart to Christ, precedes catechesis, the sharing of one's faith. Adults, like their kids, can sit through instructional classes, but until they turn their hearts to Christ and share that with others, they have experienced neither conversion nor catechesis.

In giving attention to the individual, it should not be overlooked that the recipient of catechesis is the whole Christian community and every person in it. (General Directory for Catechesis, article 168).

Religion can become merely an object to study

Third, because of the schoolhouse framework's association with general curriculum schooling, teachers working within that framework may become so concerned about covering all the facts, about teaching so much about religion, that the learner never actually meets Christ. But a person is not saved by facts about religion. One can study Islam, for example, and know its history, sacred writings, and key figures, but that would not make one a Muslim. Knowing about religion is not the same as experiencing the presence of the risen Christ and turning one's heart over to Christ through belief. Whole community catechesis remedies this, as we shall see presently.

The problem of graduation is critical

Fourth, there is the obvious problem of graduation, which is implied and expected in the schoolhouse framework. It's hard to overcome this problem. Whole community catechesis, by definition, corrects the idea that sharing one's faith, or engaging in catechesis, ever ends. Even if we believe that the schoolhouse framework is so important that we decide to retain it, the problem of graduation remains a fatal flaw in this approach.

The classroom format resists spontaneity

And fifth, the schoolhouse framework, built as it is on classrooms and teachers, does not allow a sense of the wider community to emerge. The wider community has celebration and singing and storytelling at its heart. While the classrooms work quite well for the purpose of instruction in the faith, they resist the larger experience of transformation and celebration which are also an essential aspect of catechesis. Classrooms are not an easy place for folks to share in liturgical events, not a comfortable place for visitors to be present, even parents. They tend to resist being open. Indeed, most classroom doors are closed during the class period. And finally, classrooms are usually not a good place to share food—but how can Christians expect the risen Lord to be present if there is no food to share?

And because the number of catechists needed to sustain the schoolhouse framework is so great, we do not rely enough on the gift of teaching as it is found in our communities. Teaching is a gift of the Holy Spirit. Many well-meaning catechists who do come forward do not see this work as their vocation. They see themselves as "temporaries." They're filling in a gap in the program by volunteering for a year or two as catechists. They have big hearts, free time, and often kids in the program themselves, but they do not always have the gift of teaching.

Whole community catechesis, in most cases, surfaces lead or master catechists who genuinely do experience the gift of teaching in their lives. And whole community catechesis also urges parishes to adopt more of an assembly approach than a classroom one, where liturgical celebration, visitors, shared food, and a sense of the wider community are more possible. An entire section of this manual is devoted to laying out some of these possibilities.

Summary

The schoolhouse framework, within which we provide most religious education in the U.S. church today, has some strengths. It's a good way to provide a comprehensive and systematic educational course about the church, its history, rituals, and leadership. It's a good way to bring dedicated catechists into close contact with small groups of students.

But it also has weaknesses. It may sometimes lack an essential link with the liturgy, especially the Sunday assembly. It may lack the participation of the total parish, the wider community, leaving most religious education in the hands of a tiny minority of community members. It may not provide as effective a context for faith-sharing as it does for learning about faith. The problem of graduation, real or perceived, is possibly fatal to that framework in terms of our desire to promote catechesis as lifelong and constitutive for Christians. And finally, it may not provide the learning environment most conducive to growth in faith, to the spontaneity involved in that, and to the serendipitous gifts of the Holy Spirit, especially the gift of teaching.

2

An Overview of Whole Community Catechesis

A new framework

Whole community catechesis, in sum, is a new framework within which we can provide religious education at the parish level. It begins with a renewed way of thinking about the process of sharing faith within the community. This new way has a fresh set of hoped-for outcomes. And, of course, it has a new way of doing the actual tasks, a different daily routine for the parish director of religious education, the catechists, those in support roles, and other parish leaders.

Let's take a moment here to look in brief at the planks used to build the framework called "whole community catechesis."

framework *noun.*
1. A structure for supporting or surrounding a building or program.
2. A fundamental structure, a system of ideas and approaches.
3. A consistent way of thinking or acting that follows certain inner principles which unite all aspects of a program.
4. A paradigm.

Plank #1: A link to the whole community and the Sunday assembly

The first plank of this new framework is that in whole community catechesis, the total parish is involved in learning and sharing about the faith. Every Christian of every age in the parish is involved, not just children. The Sunday assembly at Mass is the font from which all this flows. It's the font from which the whole community draws the sweet water of faith-sharing and self-understanding as the Body of Christ and the People of God.

Whole community catechesis provides a framework within which such parish-wide faith-sharing happens every single week, year in and year out. "How will you get people to actually do this?" you ask. The beauty of whole community catechesis is that it is made simple. It's in plain English. And it's delivered in small, bite-sized chunks. People will do it because it is sweet for them, because it fulfills a desire they have for the spiritual life, because it is designed to fit naturally into their everyday lives.

We're in the opening section of this manual, where all we're providing is an overview. An entire step-by-step process is laid out in this manual to show how to implement this first feature. See chapter three and appendix one for much more on this.

Plank #2: Christian households of faith and the parish as resource center

The second plank of this new framework is that the households of the parish become the main focus of re-designed parish programs. The household is where faith is lived every day. So, in whole community catechesis there is a strong focus on developing households. Eucharist extends to the home, reconciliation is practiced at home, even initiation becomes part of home life. Marriage is already there, of course, but healing and prayer become more and more home-based, too. Home is where faith is lived and shared—by grandparents, parents, children, youth, single adults, and households of all sorts.

Christian homemaking becomes very important. The household is the context in which whatever we teach in religious education class becomes the stuff of real, everyday living.

The parish programs don't go away, of course. Within the framework of whole community catechesis, the parish, in fact, becomes a more important resource center for the household than ever before! (1) The parish provides the Sunday assembly, first and foremost, the richest resource available. (2) It also provides catechetical assemblies of one kind or another, sometimes in classroom settings, but more and more beyond the classroom in gatherings or assemblies of various kinds. (More on this later!) It also provides a center for pastoral care, for the movements for justice and peace, and for personal spiritual growth. See chapter six and appendices two and three for much more on this.

This is indeed a new framework. For decades now, since the close of Vatican II, we've come to see the members of the parish as a resource pool for parish needs and ministries. They are expected to give their "time, talent, and treasure" for parish needs. And, in fact, parish schedules generally ask people to leave their homes and be present to serve at the parish site precisely during those few precious "free" hours when the family would normally gather at home.

household *noun.*
1. The person or group of people who occupy a single dwelling, including family members and hangers-on.
2. In a wider sense, the community of people who have regular contact with each other and share meals, even if not living in the same house.

But in whole community catechesis we are saying that, in fact, the opposite is true. The church is the people of God, gathered and living wherever they are. The parish is actually a resource to the church! Parish staff provide the resources that parishioners need to experience Christ more fully, to share that faith, to worship accordingly, to work for justice and peace, and to care for the poor and sick and imprisoned.

The church is, indeed, the people of God living in their own homes and neighborhoods, attending their workplaces and schools, engaging in commerce in local shopping malls, downtowns, and corner stores. The people of God, the church, gathers in all kinds of places. Fundamentally, the church gathers every night for supper. And, secondarily, it assembles at the parish church. But it also gathers in bars, clubs, restaurants, fast food joints, hospitals, morgues, support groups, and malls. When a Christian goes into one of these gatherings, bringing the love and peace of the risen Lord with him or her, everything changes. The world is brighter and more loving and blessed.

The goal of whole community catechesis is focused at the point where people actually live their lives. It seeks to deepen and enrich people's faith so that the church is wherever they are.

The parish is a reflection of the people of God, the church. It's a gathering place of the highest order. The parish is a sign of unity, of God's unending love. It's a resource center for the church. But our goal is not to build up splendid parishes and parish buildings and endowment funds. Our goal is to animate the world with the Spirit of Christ. Whole community catechesis leans into that goal in realistic and doable ways.

This manual devotes an entire section to unfolding ways to support and affirm people in their everyday living—and so to enrich life with the Spirit of Christ. See chapter five and appendices two, three, and four for much more on this.

Plank #3: A constitutive part of Christian life

The third plank in the framework of whole community catechesis also involves a change from the present way of thinking. Whole community catechesis is not an optional parish program for which one enrolls and pays tuition to participate. Catholics don't "enroll" for the Sunday assembly at Mass or "pay tuition" to participate there. Whole community catechesis starts with the premise that faith formation or learning about the faith is part and parcel of being Christian. It isn't optional. It's central, like being in the Sunday assembly at Mass.

The slightly more complex term we use to describe this is constitutive. Catechesis or growing in one's faith is constitutive, we would say, of the Christian life. One simply cannot say that he or she is a Christian unless he or she is also in a process of sharing

constitutive *adj.*
1. Making a thing what it is.
2. Being essential.
3. Having the power to establish someone for who he or she is in essence.

faith. Sharing one's faith *is* catechesis. And sharing faith, or catechesis, is what makes a Christian a Christian.

So catechesis for the whole community is not optional. But it also is not mandatory, any more than being in the Sunday assembly for Mass is truly mandatory. You really can't mandate that people share their faith. But by fitting itself into the way everyday life is lived, whole community catechesis becomes a magnet. People desire to grow spiritually, and the whole community catechesis movement helps them do that.

In this way, whole community catechesis responds to people's real, inborn hunger to be with God. It trusts people in that journey. The people of God themselves, it must be said, are a diverse, inclusive bunch! They're naturally ecumenical. They live in all sorts of domestic relationships. They follow their hearts and consciences in their journey with Christ, with the parish as their guide and gathering place.

Plank #4: A movement within God's people and the vision of the leaders

The fourth plank of whole community catechesis is that it is more like a movement within the parish than a program. In a sense, the church itself is really a movement more than it is a "membership organization." It's a movement of the Spirit of Jesus to the world. The church is a movement within our own hearts. Faith is constantly growing and changing. It's constantly in movement.

In the same way that the schoolhouse framework within which we provide catechesis has certain elements that are lacking, the membership framework within which we understand the church lacks a vital element. The membership framework suggests a sort of club mentality in which members have certain benefits that outsiders don't have. This can lead to an "us and them" attitude. But grace, we know, is not restricted to Christians, and certainly not to Catholics. The benefit is not so much that we get some divine gift which no one else gets, as that we are given a mission which is to move out to those around us and tell the Good News: the reign of God is among us. Everyone is welcome here. Everyone is offered a place at the table. Forgiveness is possible. Love your enemies. Be generous with your money. Follow the Spirit who is leading you.

To become a Christian, in short, is to join a movement, not a club. It's an unending process of announcing the Good News and assisting folks to live by it.

So, too, with whole community catechesis. It is a renewal move-

> **membership**
> *noun.*
> 1. The state of being a member.
> **movement** *noun.*
> 1. The act or instance of moving.
> 2. A series of actions and events taking place over a period of time which work to foster a principle or policy.
> 3. An organized effort by supporters of a common goal.

ment toward faith-sharing and instruction in the faith. This faith-sharing and instruction is unending and present everywhere in our lives.

As such, working within the framework of whole community catechesis serves to tie together (1) all the formal instruction which the parish provides (homilies, children's instructional programs, sacramental preparation, leadership training, preparation for various pastoral care and liturgical ministries, biblical study, and spiritual growth opportunities) with (2) the informal sharing of faith which whole community catechesis implants into everything else, especially everyday household and parish life.

The single factor which makes renewal movements (such as TEC, Search, Marriage or Engaged Encounter, Cursillo, RENEW, AA, Al Anon, and others) work is that the people involved in these movements share their lives of faith together. This gives them a feeling of movement, from one person to another, from one community to another. The Spirit moves people where the Spirit wills.

As with any movement, parish leaders must embrace whole community catechesis and bring energy and enthusiasm to it. The vision of sharing faith together as a means of experiencing ongoing conversion is the backbone of whole community catechesis. If parish leaders have turned their own hearts to Christ (conversion), and if they have shared that with others (catechesis), then they will see the essential or constitutive nature of inviting the entire parish to engage in faith-sharing at every opportunity, week in and week out.

> **catechesis** *noun.*
> 1. To echo the faith in one's own life by sharing it with others.
> 2. When done in a systematic way, it is also called instruction in the faith.

In a sense, it's similar to two other movements within any parish: (1) the movement for justice and peace and (2) the movement we call the Sunday assembly for Mass.

The movement for justice and peace depends upon the Spirit moving in people's hearts and gathering or assembling them to work together to build the city of God. If such a movement ever became a program, it would be ruined. It would lose its Spirit-driven zeal and energy.

The same is true for the Sunday assembly for Mass. The Spirit draws us there, not the rules of the church. It is the Spirit who kindles the fire within our hearts and causes us to pray together. It is in the Spirit that we depart from that assembly to our homes and workplaces, empowered to know, love, and serve the Lord and one another.

A word of caution

We are very committed to programs in the American church. They are comfortable to us because they can be defined and funded. We can write job descriptions about how to run them. We can write budgets about how to pay for them. But the life of faith, following the Way of Christ, is really quite spontaneous. It really is a movement much more than a program. The Spirit seems to ebb and flow in our lives, inspiring us toward this and urging us toward that. The Spirit of Christ, we know, cannot easily be contained or defined.

Life is like that, too. We have up times and down times. We have happy times and sad times. There is death everywhere, and then it's followed by a surprising uprising of life in its place. It flows. Life is a movement, not a program.

Whole community catechesis cannot be completely defined or predicted. Moving into it requires some risk of not knowing where it will all lead. Like Abraham and Sarah, like Moses and Miriam and Aaron, like Mary and Joseph—you really can't predict where the Spirit will move you. The idea behind whole community catechesis is to allow this movement of the Spirit to guide us.

Not to worry, we'll maintain our programs! We won't have to give up all our anchors. But within those programs, whole community catechesis adds an element of surprise and delight: a space within which the Spirit can really move us.

Summary: adult Christians of mature faith

Cullen Schippe, the publisher at Benziger, has summed this up for everyone. In whole community catechesis, he says, the new goal or outcome is "adult Christians of mature faith," following the Way of Christ, sharing supper and Eucharist, working hard for justice and peace, and turning their hearts to Christ over and over again throughout their lives. It's an entirely new framework within which the faith is shared and passed from one generation to the next. New wine, new wineskins.

As with any change in a framework, this new thinking is challenging for people who are working day-in-and-day-out in the present schoolhouse framework for religious education. It's very tough to work in one framework while building another. The house can get quite messy. But it can and must be done.

You might be wondering to yourself, "But what does this look like? What actually happens? What are the programs like? Who meets where and who does what?" These specifics of whole community catechesis will emerge as you read forward through this manual. Let's go!

Nuts & Bolts

3

Step One:
Linking Liturgy and Catechesis

Catechesis is gradual and ongoing; it takes place in and through the Christian community in the context of the liturgical year and is solidly supported by celebrations of the word.

Kate Dooley, OP
"Evangelization and Catechesis: Partners in the New Millennium,"
in *The Echo Within*

Introduction

Re-joining liturgy and catechesis in your parish is the first necessary step in implementing whole community catechesis. This may require that parish staff people, who sometimes fight over turf within the parish, first sit down together and be reconciled. It will certainly require that all share the same vision of liturgy and catechesis and the relationship between them.

There are three aspects to the re-joining of liturgy and catechesis. The first is to establish a process, given below, for allowing the liturgy to become the font from which all catechesis flows within the parish. The second is to examine the "guest list" to see who is welcome and who is excluded from the Sunday assembly. And the third is to raise the status of baptism and people's everyday experience of being baptized in Christ.

First and foremost, of course, as mentioned earlier in this manual, it's necessary to make the Sunday assembly the single most important focus of the parish week. Nothing in the parish is more important than what happens at the Sunday assembly for Mass. Christ is present there in a fourfold way: in the bread and wine, in the person of the presider, in the community which gathers, and in the Word of God which is broken open and shared (Vatican II: *The Constitution on the Sacred Liturgy*, article 7).

But for many people, Sunday Mass, and especially the readings and homily, comes and goes too quickly. Before they know it, they're back in their cars heading out for their Sunday activities. If you asked on Monday morning what the Liturgy of the Word was all about the day before, many would be hard pressed to remember.

And for many others, they simply aren't present every week for the Sunday assembly.

So how is it possible to make this the focal point of parish life? How is it possible to argue that all catechesis flows from the liturgy, from the Word of God broken open and shared in the Sunday assembly? If people aren't present, or if they are not able to take this Word with them into their weeks, how can catechesis be effective?

One: Reflection on the Sunday readings—parish-wide faith-sharing!

One solution to this is to organize a weeklong period of reflection on the Word of God shared at Sunday Mass. As we said above, sharing one's own faith is catechesis. To be a catechist is to echo the Word in one's life, and to share it with others. In the RCIA, a term is used to describe this kind of reflection on the mysteries of the faith—an ancient name which comes from the early church, *mystagogia*. (It's from the Greek language.) In plain English we call it simply, "reflecting on the mysteries of the faith."

The idea is this. What we do at Mass can become mere routine if it's celebrated frequently and without enough post-celebration reflection. But if we pause afterward to reflect on what just happened, we consolidate it all and allow it to enter more deeply into our inner life, our soul, our sense of the holy. By pausing even a little while to turn our minds back to what just happened, we will notice a line from the homily, a phrase in one of the prayers, the experience of receiving communion that touched us. We will recall a hymn melody, or a whiff of candle wax that caught our imagination in a particular way. Likewise the readings from Scripture: how did they resonate within us? How did they touch our hearts?

If all we do is "attend" Mass and then run off to a busy week without pausing, we do not allow the Word of God to penetrate us. A week of faith-sharing on the Sunday readings, though, will change everything!

Here's how it works. In the Liturgy of the Word at Mass, the homilist leads everyone, including him or herself, to ask a single, well-focused, real-life, and significant question, prompted by the scriptural text of the day. Normally, the homily proceeds as usual but leads, in the end, to a key question which those present can reflect on. It should be a question that leads to theological reflection without being too theological itself. Not a question with a "yes" or "no" response, but one that draws the believer more deeply into the Gospel, a question that asks for a personal response. It's not a discussion about the faith but a sharing of one's own faith and belief.

Question. *noun.*
1. An expression of inquiry that invites or calls for a reply.
2. An idea raised for consideration by an assembly.
3. An inquiry that leads one to a deeper understanding and personal application of truth.

For example, recently the Gospel passage for a particular Sunday was from the Sermon on the Mount in Matthew, where Jesus taught the Beatitudes. The Question of the Week posed in the homily was "Which one of these Beatitudes caught your ear this morning, and how will you allow it to affect your life more profoundly?" This is an excellent question for faith-sharing because it asks people to look into their own hearts.

A poor question for that reading would have been, "What did Jesus mean when he said, 'Blessed are the poor'?" Such a question leads to speculative theological debates about what was in Jesus' heart when he taught this. Who in the world knows the answer to that? Besides, that question does not lead to personal reflection.

During the following week, the Question of the Week is used throughout the parish for faith-sharing at the beginning of each gathering: when the staff gathers for its weekly meeting, when the choir gathers to rehearse, when the finance committee gets together on Tuesday night, before every session of religious education during the week, when the money counters do their work on Monday morning, when the classes meet in school, and when families are driving home, having supper, or finding a few moments to talk. Everyone who gathers in the parish shares faith flowing from the previous Sunday's liturgy.

This begins the catechetical process for everyone in the parish.

The parish staff (gladly) stops spending all afternoon preparing and printing "prayer services" for parish evening meetings. Instead, group members pause (as I'm describing it here) at the outset of their gathering, to listen again to the Gospel from the previous Sunday, and then to remember what has happened in their lives within the past couple of days.

Then they share that around the table. And the most amazing thing begins to happen. Solidarity begins emerging as everyone in the parish shares the same Gospel story all week long. It begins to feel as though the Gospel, once the business only of the homilist, is now everyone's business. People naturally begin to see the hand of God in their lives. And most importantly, individually and communally, folks echo the faith in their own lives and hear the echo of it in the lives of their mates.

I sat in on a finance committee at a local parish one evening. The reading for the previous Sunday was from John's Gospel where Jesus is telling his disciples that he will be leaving them. The Question of the Week was, "What is your experience of people coming into your life for a while and then leaving again?"

I'll never forget what one member of the committee shared that night.

> Well, yesterday afternoon our daughter, Sonya, moved out of our house. (A pause.) To be honest, it was a hard day for

Joanie and me. She's our youngest. And she's our baby. And she moved to Duluth, which feels like the other side of the planet to us. I helped her pack the car. I checked the oil and the tires (twice), and then we said our good-byes.

But after she was gone, and we went back into the big, quiet house, I realized that I didn't tell her what I wanted to before she pulled out. I don't know why. I'm just not that good at it, you know. In my business, you don't show your feelings that much. But I should have told her how much I love her, and I didn't. Last night lying in bed I thought, "What if something happens to her? It'll be too late." So this morning I called her. I said, "Sonnie, I've got something to tell you. I love you more than life itself, honey. I just wanted you to know that."

Pause. Everyone in the room was catechized by this banker. Without a textbook or a discussion guide, his experience served to teach the others in profound ways. It did what no book or sermon or adult education class could ever have done. It's "natural adult education." Parish members become the facilitators of it for each other.

But what if they hadn't stopped to allow for this? What if they'd just rushed into the agenda that evening in the interest of getting the work done and getting home; "it's just a finance committee," after all? What if they'd just read through a prayer service with no reflection on life? Or what if they'd said to themselves that catechesis like this is "just for kids"?! This wonderful, powerful, catechetical moment—and hundreds more like it throughout the parish—would have been missed. And what a shame that would have been.

The basis. This parish-wide sharing based on the readings and homily from the Sunday assembly is the firm basis for everything else that's done in whole community catechesis. In a sense, this is the catechetical work for the whole community.

More than one way. Some parishes prefer to do this sharing based on the readings for the upcoming Sunday liturgies. They spend the week beforehand preparing to hear the Word of God rather than spending the week afterward reflecting on what they did hear.

Here's an outline of this to aid in implementing it at your parish.

A. Develop a "Question of the Week" drawn from the Sunday readings.

- It should be a question that leads to theological reflection without being too theological itself.

- Not a question with a "yes" or "no" response, but one that draws the believer more deeply into the Gospel.

- A question that asks for a personal response. It's not a discussion about the faith but a sharing of one's own faith and belief.

- See appendix one for some suggestions on how to do this.

B. Within the parish, the homilist delivers this question each week by sharing about it him or herself as part of the homily.

- This requires a certain ending for all Sunday homilies in the parish.

- The homilist also shares from his or her own life, taking some personal risk in doing this.

C. Repeat the Question of the Week in the bulletin each week, or in a bulletin insert. Also repeat it in school bulletins, meeting agendas, and other communication tools in the parish.

- Ask each group that meets to share about this question as the opening prayer of their meeting.

- Provide a brief, one-page faith-sharing guide to help folks in the parish lead prayer using this formula. See appendix one for an example of that guide.

- Follow this four-step prayer formula:

    1) Invite everyone to pause and prepare for prayer.

    2) Re-read part or all of the Sunday Gospel.

    3) Allow about 15 minutes at the beginning of each meeting for faith-sharing based on the Question of the Week. For larger groups, ask the members to split into small groups for the sharing to keep it within 15 minutes.

    4) Close this with brief prayer.

• Suspend the use of all other opening prayers.

• Invite members of parish households to share in this same way—
it's naturally ecumenical, inclusive, and catechetical!

D. This allows the Sunday assembly to extend into the entire week
throughout the parish! It truly becomes the source of parish life.

Summary

So far we have proposed that whole community catechesis is
launched by what happens in the Sunday assembly for Mass—and the
faith-sharing done throughout the following (or previous) week,
based on the Scripture broken open by the homily.

Two: Who feels welcome at your Sunday assembly?

A short reflection on this difficult question. During the Easter season
we hear many readings in the Liturgy of the Word. Because we worship so frequently during the Triduum and early Easter season, these
many readings and stories from Sacred Scripture tend to swim together in our minds and imaginations. Even if you don't come to church
for those days, you still know what's going on there.

On Holy Thursday: the last supper, the washing of the feet, bringing into each church the oils that are blessed by the bishop and used
for anointing and baptisms.

On Good Friday: the crucifixion and death with the reading of the
passion story, the veneration of the cross. Good Friday is the one day
on which no Mass is celebrated anywhere in the world.

And then on the holiest night of the year, Holy Saturday: the Easter
Vigil. The candlelight opening, the blessing of the fire and the water,
baptism and confirmation, new members initiated into the church
community.

Easter Sunday morning: lilies, fresh water, big crowds, pink and yel-
low spring dresses, new life, a new beginning, a strong sense of opti-
mism. Alleluias are sung again!

There are two events in this whole story that swim together for me.
The first is on Holy Thursday evening at the supper meal. What strikes
me is that Jesus was the host there. It was his table, set for him. And
the second is the reading about Jesus meeting his disciples in the

upper room with Thomas doubting it all, hidden there behind their locked doors, huddled together. What struck me in the latter story was how Jesus still claimed the disciples as his own!

I mean, these people had, for the most part, run out on him in his hour of need. They were full of doubts. But to Jesus, it did not matter who they were. Forgiveness was such a strong theme of his teaching and of his practice that none of that mattered. He would still eat with them and still invite them to the banquet—that fish fry on the beach in John's Gospel, at Emmaus in Luke's Gospel, after the supper, in the upper room; let's get something to eat, he says.

Christ is the host. Christ sets the table. Christ welcomes them all! In thinking about all this, I suddenly realized that that's the Good News!

The table around which we gather does not "belong" to us. It is not set by us. We don't own it. It belongs to Christ. If we were the ones making up the guest list and setting out the meal, I suspect it would be less inclusive than Jesus' guest list. Our meal would be a little more skimpy. We tend not to forgive as easily, and we hold sins against one another. We tend to exclude others from our tables.

But the good news is that Jesus does not.

Now in the ministry of catechesis, this is a very important point. For catechesis to be successful, being in the Sunday assembly is as important as being in the catechetical assemblies on Wednesday night. Catechesis assumes participation in the whole life of the church. And yet many times throughout the church the households of the children we see in religious education are not the ones we see in the Sunday assembly. And, at least for some of them, it's because we have not made them feel very welcome and in fact, have made them feel downright unwelcome. We've made some feel unworthy, at least less worthy than the rest of us(!). And some have allowed themselves to stay away for so long that their faith is now weak, and they just don't know how to get restarted.

We should establish a policy that everyone is welcome in the Sunday assembly. And we should make that very public. We should put up billboards around our town or neighborhood announcing this Good News! "Whoever you are, whatever you've done, you are welcome here."

Nothing can separate anyone from the love of God in Christ Jesus. We all belong to Christ. In a sense, he joined us to himself by his death and resurrection. In this great paschal mystery, our hearts were made Christ's forever. We are, in short, now a part of the body of Christ, no matter what. Even, or especially, if we are outside the fold and know it.

Why would we want to exclude anyone, especially someone who desires to gather with us, from the Sunday assembly which is the place where grace is shared in such abundance?

The Litany of the Saints

Here is a litany that might be used as a welcome speech before each gathering of the faithful assembled on Sunday for Mass.

> Who are you? Are you married with kids, worrying for them and committed to their welfare? Are you divorced? Are you married for the second, or even the third time? Are you a single parent struggling to make ends meet, but also hoping to have love in your life again? Are you gay or lesbian? Well if you are, then you belong to us because you belong to Christ. The Good News is that Christ is the host here today and he welcomes you as part of his body. The words from the Gospel are addressed to you: Peace be with you.
>
> Are you lonely? Are you a widow? Are you a single man or woman who would prefer to have a spouse? Are you disabled or disfigured? Have you run out of luck? Does your life seem flat? Is your faith on a slowdown? Well, if you are, then you belong to us because you belong to Christ! The Good News is that Christ is the host here today and he welcomes you as part of his body. The words from the Gospel are addressed to you: Peace be with you.
>
> Are you struggling financially? Have you been laid off? Out of work because of downsizing? Does it seem like you can never quite get it all together? Well, if so, then you belong to us because you belong to Christ! The Good News is that Christ is the host here today and he welcomes you as part of his body. The words from the Gospel are addressed to you: Peace be with you.

Are you struggling with family-planning questions? Have you been a victim of abuse or violence, of a crime? Are you fearful? Are you a criminal or imprisoned? Do you have a past about which you feel ashamed? Are you homeless or hopeless? Well, if so, then you belong to us because you belong to Christ! The Good News is that Christ is the host here today and he welcomes you as part of his body. The words from the Gospel are addressed to you: Peace be with you.

Are you new here? An immigrant maybe? Are you from another Christian tradition? Are you full of doubt today, like Thomas? Are you fearful like the disciples were? Has it been a while since you darkened the doorway of this church? None of that matters. You belong to us because you belong to Christ. The Good News is that Christ is the host here today and he welcomes you as part of his body. The words from the Gospel are addressed to you: Peace be with you.

All people of good will are welcome here: that's the really Good News!

If you've been away, you can come back; if you've been living in darkness, you can come to the light; if you haven't been able to believe without seeing him, look around you, the Body of Christ has come to Mass today. Sinners are welcome, saints, too. Everyone is welcome to come to Christ, our Lord and our God, indeed!

Three: Raising the status of baptism

The bottom line. The success of whole community catechesis is directly linked to the place baptism holds in parish life. In many places, baptism is a "lost sacrament." It's practiced, of course, but quietly. No real exchange of promises is sought from anyone receiving it. It's often done in semi-private settings. Or if it's celebrated at Sunday Mass, it may anger parishioners who feel it makes Mass too long!

Over the years since the close of Vatican II, very little effective catechesis has been provided on baptism, with the one major exception of the Rite of Christian Initiation of Adults (and children). In the early years of the church, baptism was a major sacrament that, along with Eucharist, initiated the Christian into a life of faith. But today, baptism holds a much more minor place in most parishes. We still teach about baptism as though it's "just one of the seven sacraments." In fact, though, baptism is on a par with Eucharist and we should raise its status to reflect that.

The baptismal promises that people make are very important, but most people do not understand them. I asked one of my focus groups last year, a group of typical adult Catholics chosen by their pastoral staff, to tell me what they thought they had promised at baptism. Here's what one gentleman wrote:

To be honest, I was baptized as an infant so I don't remember. It has something to do with rejecting Satan and all that. I suppose it's a commitment to live as a loyal Christian or something. I've heard them repeated a number of times in church but they tend to go right over my head.

A bigger commitment than that! In order for whole community cate-chesis to stand on firm footing and become a lasting process of living the Christian life, like the Eucharist is, we must catechize about it with more vigor. We must be more effective in helping folks see its vital place in their lives. This is true for all of us, including adults and children.

In Sacrosanctum Concilium, the document renewing the liturgy, which was published at Vatican II, the pope and bishops spent half the document discussing the central place baptism and Eucharist have in the Christian life. Later in the document, they gave a single article each to confirmation (#71), reconciliation (#72), and holy orders (#76). Anointing and matrimony had five articles between them!

Baptism is a central Christian sacrament and ought to have a pro-gram of catechesis that is appropriate to that. In the short run, this pro-gram of catechesis must play "catch up" ball! We've gone too long without paying enough attention to it.

A focus group. I was sitting with another focus group of parents one evening at a parish, asking how to best teach about baptism to their third grade children. "How do you do it now?" one mom asked. I explained that in our textbook we had a chapter on baptism that treat-ed the history, the meaning of the symbols, and the words of the rites.

"Well," she said with a shrug in her voice, "that's your problem. You're doing it all wrong. How do you teach about birthdays?" she asked me. "You don't teach about the history of birthdays and the meaning of the symbols," she said. "No. You bake a cake and buy some presents. By the second year, the kid gets it. And they have it for life. They never lose it. You must have baptisms," she said. Of course she's right.

A rule of thumb. In order for us to raise the status of baptism, we're going to have to take certain bold and unprecedented steps. Each per-son who is in catechesis (everyone!) should have at least two full expe-riences of baptism each year. This includes preparation for the sacra-ment, the rite itself, and a follow-up mystagogia. One of these experi-ences should surely be at the Easter Vigil—but most parishioners do not attend those rites. Another option is to gather folks for the purpose of preparing, celebrating, and reflecting upon this sacrament through-out the year. See appendix five for an example of one way to do this.

Summary

So far we have proposed that (1) the Sunday assembly be the font from which the whole community draws catechesis. (2) By being made to feel welcome, even (or especially!) if they live in irregular household situations, all community members gather to share in that assembly. (3) Drawing from the homily there, all parish groups and classes, and all parish households are invited over and over and over again to share their faith with each other. And (4) all of this is situated in a deeper appreciation for being baptized, for living the paschal mystery in one's own life, dying in Christ and experiencing the wonderful sense of resurrection to which that leads for us humans.

This is the cornerstone of whole community catechesis. It's a real change in the framework within which we provide for catechesis in the parish because it's so very different from the schoolhouse framework. But just imagine a parish in which this goes on every week! Imagine the new relationships that would bud. Imagine the importance that would be attached to the Sunday assembly! Imagine how much more religious instruction, however it's provided, would be received in the hearts of those who are sharing faith already!

4

Making Christ Jesus (more) the Center of Catechesis

"The baptismal catechumenate is first and foremost about bringing participants into relationship with Jesus Christ and helping them turn to him with their whole hearts. Is this task the first priority of the catechetical programs in our parish or school?"

Christopher Weber, Archdiocese of Baltimore
NCCL *Catechetical Leadership*, Volume 12, No. 2

Prologue

The Christian journey is summarized in the Gospels and other writings of the Christian Scriptures. It's not very complicated. In plain English it can be summed up like this:

> We meet Christ.
> We turn our hearts over to Christ again and again.
> We share that in love with others, especially the poor.
> We tell those around us what we are experiencing.
> They meet Christ through us.
> They turn their hearts over to Christ again and again.
> They share that in love with others, especially the poor.
> And they tell those around them what they are experiencing.
> Before long, the whole world is saved.
> The mission of the Church is to support and sustain this in the lives of those called to be Christians.

One: Christ is the center

Here's what the *Catechism of the Catholic Church* has to say about this:

> The first and last point of reference of this catechesis will always be Jesus Christ himself, who is "the way, and the truth, and the life." (article 1698)

And here's what the early church had to say:

> "For to me, living is Christ..." (Philippians 1:21a).

And here's what *The General Directory for Catechesis* has to say (from the *GDC in Plain English*).

> Jesus Christ not only transmits God's word;
> Jesus is that word and all catechesis is completely tied to him.
> What does this mean?
> First, what we find at the heart of all catechesis is not a book or a theology system but a person!
> The fundamental task of catechesis is to present Christ and everything in relation to him, leading people to follow Christ in their lives. (article 98)

The encounter. So in catechesis, the encounter is not with a textbook, even if the student can memorize it. The encounter is not with "correct doctrine" even if the student can repeat it back to us perfectly. The encounter is with Christ through the catechist. A catechist is one who shares his or her faith, one who shares what he or she is experiencing in Christ. As the catechist shows others the Way of Christ, those others see in the catechist the very faith, charity, love, and hope which they themselves seek.

Encounter. *noun.*
1. A meeting, especially one that is unplanned or unexpected.
2. An opportunity for one to see briefly into the life of another.

Here's what Fr. John Hurley (Director of the Office for Evangelization at the U.S. bishops' national headquarters in

Washington, DC) has to say about the spirituality of those who work in catechesis.

> Why do catechists catechize? It is not just to transfer knowledge and teachings. It is to call others to be witnesses and disciples of Jesus Christ. Of course, this requires that our catechists be witnesses and disciples...If catechists have not experienced an encounter with Jesus, then how can they "talk the talk" with other people?... If they have encountered the Lord personally, then they can't keep that a secret.

Two: Conversion (turning our hearts to Christ) precedes catechesis

Conversion to Christ precedes catechesis. And once experienced, it's conversion that leads a person to undertake his or her journey of faith. A person who has not yet really met Jesus Christ and decided to follow Christ, can sit in a classroom and study religion, but until there is conversion, that person won't be a dedicated follower of Christ.

One of the difficulties (recognized by the *General Directory*) in our present method of providing religious education is that so few of those in catechesis have experienced this conversion. As a result, their hearts are often not in the program! But even more difficult, some of the catechists we recruit also have not experienced this conversion! They agree to teach fourth grade this year, for example, but they're not in it with their whole hearts. Like the kids, they may even dread the weekly classes a little. But as article 142 of the *General Directory for Catechesis* puts it:

Convert *verb.*
1. To turn around.
2. To make a fundamental shift in one's beliefs and horizons.
3. To turn and adopt a new way of viewing life and the world.

There cannot be teachers of the faith other than those who are convinced and faithful disciples of Christ and his Church.

Here's what else the *General Directory for Catechesis* says about this. There is a strong message contained in here:

> Many who present themselves for catechesis truly require genuine conversion. Because of this, the Church usually desires that the first stage in the catechetical process be dedicated to ensuring conversion…Only by starting with conversion… can catechesis, strictly speaking, fulfill its proper task…
> (The GDC, article 62)

Baptism is no guarantee. Unfortunately, baptism is no guarantee of conversion. For some, the faith begins with great vigor, but they lose heart after a while. For others, their faith was never deep; it always remained on the surface of their lives until something better or more interesting came along. And for still others, perhaps many others, baptism was just not taken very seriously to begin with! Or they were baptized as an infant, but raised in a home where faith was not part of everyday life. Consequently, these have never come to know Jesus in their own lives.

Jesus spoke of faith like this in the Gospel. The writers of the *General Directory* saw in this the seeds for everything they wrote about the renewal of catechesis in our day and age.

> A sower went out to sow. And as he sowed, some seed fell on the path, and the birds came and ate it up. Other seed fell on rocky ground, where it did not have much soil, and it sprang up quickly, since it had no depth of soil. And when the sun rose, it was scorched; and since it had no root, it withered away. Other seed fell among thorns, and the thorns grew up and choked it, and it yielded no grain. Other seed fell into good soil and brought forth grain, growing up and increasing and yielding thirty and sixty and a hundredfold. Let anyone with ears to hear listen! (Mark 4:3-8)

And here's the rub. Because the seed of faith is vulnerable to the changing soil of one's life (to borrow Jesus' metaphor a moment) the church takes great care to provide ongoing catechesis to nourish faith and help it blossom.

The catechesis which follows upon conversion requires a sort of apprenticeship in the early stages. It requires that a catechist apprentice to him or herself others who wish to know how to follow the Way of Christ. It's far more than merely teaching a "lesson in a textbook," isn't it? And they're far more than mere "students," aren't they?

It's so easy to see how all this must have conversion as a starting element!

This isn't to say that there is no place for textbook learning in helping people to understand religion and become solid Christians. The bishops of the church rightly expect us to provide a comprehensive instruction in the faith at every level of catechesis. But the textbook part must come after the conversion. It must come when one's heart is in accord with the Gospel. It must come when it has a chance of making a difference.

Three: How does a learner of any age meet Christ?

First and foremost, by sharing faith with others. Nothing can replace faith-sharing as a means to help others meet Christ. In sharing one's journey to the heart of the Lord with others, something opens up in one's own heart.

Conversion normally occurs in a communal setting. It involves people gathering with others in order to share faith in the Lord. It's a process or a movement. It can't be scheduled in the curriculum. It doesn't necessarily follow chapter 3, for example, in an orderly fashion. Does this sound a little like the catechumenate? Indeed! All we are saying here flows directly from the spirituality of the RCIA.

In this process, each person looks into the events and people of his or her life, and sees them anew as part of his or her faith. One then begins to see (slowly at first) that one must die to oneself in order to rise with happiness, and then go forth to love as a follower of Christ. Conversion of this sort is ongoing throughout life: conversion moment followed by conversion moment...

And normally, it's a shared experience, which is why it's so necessary to encourage and invite folks to share their faith with each other as often as possible.

Such faith-sharing happens in two ways. First, there is faith-sharing that flows from the Liturgy of the Word in the Sunday assembly for Mass. That sharing is explicitly about how God's movement in one's life is experienced. We've been talking here about that in chapter three.

The second sort of faith-sharing flows from another, similar inspiration, the everyday experiences of being

Share. *verb.*
1. To keep a portion for oneself while at the same time offering a portion to others.
2. To give or receive something from another.
3. To enter into a joint participation with others.

human and knowing God. There is a simple but profound question that can surface in this sharing.

> Thinking back over the moments of your life as it unfolded in the last day or two, who or what made a difference in your life? Does some specific action or event come to mind?

By naming these persons and events, we make ourselves ready to see God in them. But if we ignore them and just keep rushing through life without these sacred pauses to reflect, we miss noticing God's hand in our lives.

Here is the bottom line on this: God is acting in your life. When you can identify that and be grateful for it, then you grow closer and closer to God. And when you share that with others, a natural sort of catechesis occurs.

The question, again, is "What's happening in your life?" Have there been moments of forgiveness, generosity, love, fairness, or friendship? Have you had a lot of hard work or family meals or a failure of trust? Have you experienced hatred, revenge, greed, cheating, broken promises, betrayal, sex without commitment, or fear? Has there been relationship loss, or have your most intimate relationships been a source of joy?

Once you can name the experience itself, then you are ready to ask the second question:

> Where is God's hand in that, or why does God seem absent?

These two forms of faith-sharing work together to create an environment in which ongoing conversion can be experienced, over and over again. Therefore, before you approach the text to teach about religion, first create an environment where this kind of sharing can occur. Then when you do teach about the doctrine or liturgy or history of the church, it makes sense because it has faith as its context.

This form of faith-sharing might seem risky to us because whenever we speak of the great mysteries of life—or the ordinary events of everyday life—we always need to share our personal experiences. This personal sharing is something many people avoid. It was the feature of the old concept of the sacrament of penance that people may have disliked the most. But personal sharing about what's happening in our lives and how God is present (or seems absent) is the key to conversion. Honest, personal sharing is in part what makes Alcoholics Anonymous so successful for people. It forces us to put our whole selves on the line, which is the avenue to healing, forgiveness, and salvation.

Nothing less will do. Everyone who is truly in love with another person knows this. Every true penitent knows it. Honest, personal sharing is what opens the door to conversion in Christ, to turning our hearts to Christ who is present among us, loving us.

Of course, such honest personal sharing must be age appropriate; it must be appropriate, period. It should never become, for example, emotional exhibitionism. But risks aside, faith sharing is essential.

A second way to meet Christ is by hearing the story of someone who has faith. There comes a time in each and every religion session when it's necessary to simply stop following the textbook for a while. Not everything you teach will be found in the textbook. At some point, you must allow your disciples and apprentices to inquire into the faith themselves. What aspects of a faith life are they wondering about? What aspects of life do they wonder about?

One of the ways to encourage this wonder is to invite them to see into your own heart. How do you do that? Try this: pause in the midst of what you're teaching. Put down the textbook. Tell those around you what you believe. Tell them what you experience about the Eucharist, for example, or about forgiveness, or about justice. Your belief and your experience of the faith is a vital part of what you teach. For example, you might say:

> You know, I believe in Jesus Christ. I have been forgiven and healed by Christ in ways I did not even realize I needed healing. I've been touched by the power of Christ's hand in my own life. I have come to love Jesus and to experience his love in my own life.

And so forth. Learn to speak about your faith in your own words—and in age-appropriate ways, share that with others. The *General Directory for Catechesis* seems to encourage this:

> Nothing—not the method or the texts, or any other part of the

program is more important than the person of the catechist in every phase of the catechetical process.

The gifts given to the catechist by the Spirit to witness faithfully and live accordingly are the very soul of catechetical ministry. (article 156, *The GDC in Plain English*)

The *General Directory for Catechesis* affirms that catechist formation should help them learn how to speak about their faith.

The formation of catechists will prepare them to share their own faith in Jesus and lead others to entrust themselves to Jesus.

The absolute summit and center of catechetical formation lies in learning how to communicate the Gospel message effectively.

Jesus Christ is the center of this—it is Christ whom we communicate to others and the catechist must be able to animate the journey to Christ which those in his or her care are making.

Toward this end, then, the catechist will be prepared to proclaim Christ, the first step, but also to make known the story of Christ as a story of salvation.

The catechist will also lead those being catechized to know Jesus Christ as the Son of God and to desire the union with Christ which the sacraments of initiation celebrate.

All the rest of catechesis is a deepening of this first journey. (article 235, *The GDC in Plain English*)

Third, for almost all Catholics, another way of meeting Christ is a sacramental experience. We come to terms with how we must die in Christ through baptism and reconciliation. We find within ourselves a profound desire for communion with Christ and those we love. We experience healing and peace. And we feel the same excitement that those first apostles must have felt as we go forth now, confirmed in the faith, eager to tell others the good news!

In the sacraments, all the faith we share comes together in a single moment of celebration! The dying and rising of Christ becomes real for us, and it becomes part and parcel of our own journey.

Fourth, in meeting the poor and the rejected, and in learning to love them, one comes very close to the heart of the Lord. How we treat the imprisoned, how we turn the other cheek, how we share our own wealth with those in need—this is how we truly know that conversion is occurring in our lives. The poor and rejected will shape our lives, just as they did Jesus'.

How we treat the poor and rejected is the measuring stick by which we will be judged. For Jesus and his followers, the poor are not just one theme among many. The poor help us understand the Gospel as the Good News of liberation (blessed are you who are poor). The poor stand as the final criteria of salvation or damnation. It is useless to belong to the Roman Catholic Church, to have all the means of salvation, to submit ourselves heart and mind to the hierarchical system, to take unto ourselves all revealed truths, unless we have love, for without love we are nothing (1 Corinthians 13:2).

> Come to me, blessed of my Father, take possession of the Kingdom prepared for you since the creation of the world (Matthew 25:34), because when you do this to one of these least ones, you did this to me (Matthew 25:45).

The question of the poor is so essential to the tradition of Jesus, that when Paul went to verify his doctrine before the apostles in

Jerusalem, they required that he care for the poor (Galatians 2:10).

The theological tradition of the church has always correctly argued that where Christ is, there too is the church. Christ is in the poor; so the church must also be in the poor. Not only in the poor who happen to be good workers, but also purely and completely in those people who are simply poor. By being poor, they are aware, as we all must be, that they have a great need for Christ's message. For this reason they are the first recipients of this good news and the first who benefit from the liberating intervention of the God of life.

Summary

So far we have proposed that (1) the Sunday assembly be the font from which the whole community draws catechesis. (2) By being made to feel welcome, even (or especially!) if they live in irregular household situations, all community members gather to share in that assembly. (3) Drawing from the homily there, all parish groups and classes, and all parish households are invited over and over and over again to share their faith with each other. And (4) all of this is situated in a deeper appreciation for being baptized. In baptism we die to ourselves in Christ and have the chance to live in the happiness of the resurrection. We learn to "live our baptisms" in everyday life.

Then in this chapter we have proposed that Christ be more and more the center of all catechesis. In this section we said that (1) turning our hearts to Christ, over and over again throughout our lives, precedes learning about our faith. (2) We turn our hearts to Christ by (a) sharing our faith, no matter how new or weak, with others, (b) hearing the witness of those who know Christ, (c) celebrating the sacraments with the rest of the church, and (d) meeting Christ in the poor and rejected of our society and world.

5

Making the Household the Focus of Catechesis

"Won't you stay for supper?"
The Christian greeting that matters most.

The role of the household in catechesis

The good old days. It's a relatively recent phenomenon in the church that so much of catechesis is done by catechists outside the home. For many generations, Catholic parents taught their children by both example and instruction at home. They prayed as families, kneeling on their living room floors, rosaries in hand. They filled their houses with sacramentals, signs of the faith. They scheduled their lives using a calendar with the saints and feast days. They observed Sunday as a holy day of rest. They fulfilled their duties to attend Mass, confess sins, and follow the rules of the church. They married mainly other Catholics, "mixed marriages" being the exception. And they lived in an American Catholic subculture, following laws on fasting and abstinence, and observing mid-week feast days despite the more widespread Protestant culture. There were Catholic Boy Scout troops, Catholic mothers of the year, Catholic schools and hospitals and funeral parlors and cemeteries—neighborhoods where one could grow up and never leave the Catholic culture.

Whatever happened in catechism class beyond this "Catholic cultural life" was not expected to fill in very many gaps. Parents, as the marriage rite dictated, were expected to raise their kids in the faith, even if one of the parents wasn't Catholic.

We can't go backward. It isn't possible or desirable to go back to those years in the American church. They were a phenomenon that emerged partly from being a community of immigrants at the time, partly from the thinking prevalent then that Protestants were "heretics," and partly from the Catholic piety that resulted from the renewal following the Council of Trent in the 16th century.

As that period waned very rapidly in the 1960s, the present practice evolved. The household became almost entirely disengaged from providing a cultural Catholic setting. Catholicism and other Christian faiths became more similar. In the late 1960s, Catholics in America passed through a period of serious disagreement with the Roman authorities of the church over birth control. Families were challenged by the rise of cultural icons like television. They no longer prayed together at home as much. They no longer followed a strict observance of feast days, fasting, and church rules. In fact, they no longer even sat down to supper together as often as they used to—in some cases, they stopped doing so altogether.

During this period, parents started dropping their kids off for CCD class while they went grocery shopping. The expectation slowly arose for many that it was up to the parish to provide faith formation. But we all know the truth. A child comes to a parish religious education program an hour a week, or twenty minutes a day in a Catholic school. No matter how good the program or textbook may be, if that child returns home to a household where no faith is shared, then there's very little the catechist or schoolteacher can do for that child's faith.

It's not a matter of learning the catechism. Remember, that was a small part of Catholic formation, even in those "good old days." It's a matter of meeting Christ, turning one's heart to Christ, living in Christ's love, and telling others about that. Conversion and catechesis entail learning a way of life, the Way of Christ. The disciple slowly grows in the ability to pray. He or she learns to see the world through the lens of the Gospel. The disciple identifies her or himself as a Christian, living counter to the dominant culture of the times.

Furthermore, regardless of what else we think we're doing in our religious education programs, the households in which our learners live are already the most influential factor in their formation. This is true about their religious beliefs as well as other aspects of life: values, dreams, and lifestyle. An hour a week in our programs simply can't compete with the rest of life.

The lived faith experience going on in most of the households in our parishes can actually contribute tremendously to the formation of the children who live there, if it is made more explicit and seen as catechetical in nature. Such natural household catechesis is the mainstay for growing in the Christian life, not merely supplemental to a parish program.

Without for a moment hoping for or trying to orchestrate any sort of return to the pre-Vatican II church, whole community catechesis does rely on a certain level of Christian homemaking.

Here's what the *Declaration on Christian Education* from Vatican II had to say about this (from *Vatican II in Plain English*).

> Parents are, in fact, the first and foremost educators of their children within a family atmosphere animated with love providing a well-rounded formation.
>
> The family can be called the first school of those social virtues which every society needs.
>
> The Christian family is enriched by the grace of the sacrament of matrimony and is the place where children are first taught to know and love God and to know and love their neighbor.
>
> Here they come to understand human companionship, here they're introduced into civic life, and here initiated into the parish community. (from article 3)

Here's what the *Catechism of the Catholic Church* says on this topic.

> Parents have the first responsibility for the education of their children. They bear witness to this responsibility first by creating a home where tenderness, forgiveness, respect, fidelity, and disinterested service are the rule. (from article 2223)
>
> Family catechesis precedes, accompanies, and enriches other

forms of instruction in the faith. (from article 2226)

And, of course, the *General Directory* agrees.

The family is defined by Vatican II as a domestic church....

The family passes on human values in the Christian tradition, and it awakens a sense of God in its youngest members.

It teaches the first tentative steps of prayer, it forms the moral conscience, and it teaches human love as a reflection of divine love.

Indeed, the catechetics of the home are more witness than teaching, more occasional than systematic, and more daily than structured into periods.

(article 255, *The GDC in Plain English*)

Four steps

Whole community catechesis might unfold more easily if the following four steps were followed in the parish. First, employ a method to involve the households of the parish on at least a 50-50 basis. Second, establish a process whereby leaders in the parish formally listen to the needs of the households. Third, begin to teach Christian homemaking as part of parish life. And finally, shift away from the schoolhouse framework within which religious instruction is offered, to a framework more friendly to parents, grandparents, older siblings, hangers-on, and all other parishioners.

In this chapter, we're going to consider the first three of these steps. Chapter six deals exclusively with the fourth step.

But first, we must start with ourselves. First and foremost, we in religious education must believe that the role of the household is on a par with our own efforts. This is humbling for us. It means that, regarding the households of the parish, for example, it isn't so much that they volunteer to help us as that we are helping them do their work. We are their servant, their resource center, their cheerleader.

Here's what one parish director told me last year:

I'll be honest. At first, I did not like either of these ideas, that my program is not the most important thing going, or that my approach might have to widen to include the whole community.

With regard to the first, I thought to myself, I work damn hard and I don't especially like being told that what I'm doing is ineffective. I used to wonder why these families can't get it through their thick skulls that they should turn off the TV and spend time with their kids. But then one night driving home at 9:45 PM after yet another night on duty at the parish, I realized that I had not seen my own kids for two whole days! I almost drove off the road! It hit me like a ton of bricks.

So the next day I decided to talk to my staff about this—and it turns out they were having the same experience, all except the sister on our staff, but even she never sees her community.

OK, I said to myself, this is bad. How can I change it?

And this opened the door for me to start taking a look at this idea of engaging the whole parish more. What surprised me is that, as we started moving on this whole community idea, I realized that I would actually have more time for my family! I would also have much less hassle trying to recruit and train all those volunteers for all those classrooms.

So I felt like St. Paul. I had a vision on the road. Go figure!

Step One: Catechesis on a 50-50 basis

It's already happening! When parents and children express their love and affection for each other—with notes, hugs, or other signs of kindness, catechesis can occur. All that's needed is for these acts to become an explicit part of their Christian life.

When family members care for each other when sick, notice when someone is lonely, affirm each other for jobs well done, and pay attention to the poor of the world, catechesis can occur. Let these become teaching moments within the household. Coach parents and guardians to make them explicit.

When a household cares for the environment and recycles all they can, catechesis can occur. Use these moments to teach about creation and ecology and the connection between the two.

When a household decides together how much to contribute to the parish or to the poor, catechesis can occur. Think of this as a natural moment to teach about stewardship and why they practice it.

When a household sits down to a meal together, pausing to enjoy each other and their food, and paying attention to one another's lives, catechesis can occur. When family members forgive each other freely, when reconciliation is a natural part of household life, catechesis can occur.

And yes, when the members of a household talk explicitly about their faith, catechesis can occur. This is a chance to view what's happening in the world around them with Christian insight: capital punishment cases, rumors of war, generous public charity, the presence of many faiths, death, loss, love, and beauty.

When a household is present together in the Sunday assembly, or visits an ailing relative, or takes a vacation together, catechesis can occur.

Already underway but not yet affirmed. These are all ways of living that are already underway in many of the households of every single parish. No one has to organize this. All that is needed is to affirm and support it. But how?

Let's make a deal. Why not enter into a 50-50 Plan with the households of the parish? In this, invite each household (which might include parents, guardians, partners, children, grandparents, other family members, or even guests and hangers-on) to take a direct role in living a Christian way of life, and in teaching others within the household to do the same.

In this way, the parish takes seriously and trusts the household. It's a method for opening up the shared responsibility for passing on the faith. If you use the catechesis assemblies described in chapter six, this will be easier to do. But even if you keep the classroom approach, this method of sharing the responsibility works beautifully.

In this plan, the parish makes some serious promises: to provide religious instruction classes, a fine Sunday assembly, and an open door to the households of faith they serve. By making such promises, the 50-50 Plan shapes the parish itself, making it more responsive to what the households of the parish need and want in order to live their faith more fully.

Likewise, the household (no matter how it's comprised) makes some serious promises as well: to use the ordinary events of everyday Christian life as catechesis. Hence, the 50-50 Plan also shapes the households and provides ongoing and deep renewal of heart throughout the parish.

Everybody learns and everybody wins.

More specifically, here's an example of what the parish might promise. Any given parish may promise all these things, or some of them, or others which fit into their culture and parish spirit.

- As a parish we promise to offer solid preaching and an opportunity for faith-sharing based on the Sunday readings every week.

- We promise to offer a weekly catechesis class or assembly, well-planned and well-coordinated and at no direct cost to the household.

- We promise that those who come from your household to the catechesis assemblies will receive sound instruction about the fundamentals of the Christian faith. We'll use instructional materials approved by the local bishop, and we'll provide lead catechists who are well prepared for their work, and who truly "echo the faith" in their own lives.

- From time to time, we'll offer evening or Saturday programs to assist you as a household in living your faith more openly and explicitly, especially during Advent and Lent.

- We promise to help you find ways as a household to serve the poor, the rejected, and the suffering; if you wish, we will coach you on how to visit the sick, the imprisoned, the lonely, and the refugee.

- We further promise to make the Sunday assembly the single most important focal point of parish life. We'll prepare for it carefully and help you as a household to be well disposed for it, ready to participate, and actively engaged in the rites.

- We'll welcome you to our Sunday assembly regardless of your situation in life, whether you're single, widowed, divorced, remarried, in an ecumenical or interfaith marriage, gay or lesbian, or sharing a home without marriage; whether you're an immigrant or a newcomer; whether you're fully abled or handicapped, healthy or sick, old or young; whether you're struggling with your faith or firm in your commitment. We'll maintain an open door and an open heart to you, and we'll offer you a share in the grace of Christ which fills this church.

- If you call us for help, we'll do everything possible to provide it to you. If you call with a question, we'll answer promptly. If you ask for prayer, we'll offer it immediately.

- In general, we're here for you, to help deepen and affirm your faith and your way of life. We promise to assemble each Sunday to celebrate the Lord's Supper and to welcome you to join us. Beyond that, we promise to provide the resources you need to help guide the disciples within your household to the Christian Way of Life.

And on the other hand, here's an example of what each household might promise. Again, any given household may choose some or all of these, or other things not on this sample list but which fit into their household culture or spirit.

- We promise to become more intentional Christian homemakers by paying attention to what happens in our home regarding meals, prayer, and time spent together. We will share our faith in our household, following the direction given by the Question of the Week in the parish.

- We promise to share love openly (exchange love notes, gifts, and other signs of affection) and to pay attention to one another's daily activities.

- At least once each week, we promise to spend time (with the TV off) compiling a family scrapbook and photo album containing bits and pieces from the people and events of our household.

- We promise to have supper together as often as possible, adding a bit of romance to our table (candlelight, wine, and flowers). We'll do this at least twice each week, and always on Sundays.

- If there's a quarrel in our household, we promise to work for reconciliation that is explicit and expressed in words such as "I am sorry" and "I forgive you."

- We promise to become more conscious of those people in our family, neighborhood, parish, or wider society whom we dislike or hate; to publicly forgive them for any harm done to us and to find ways to be more tolerant of people we don't like; to gossip less and affirm more.

- At least once each week we promise to read a newspaper together as a household and become explicitly aware of people who are suffering from war, poverty, exploitation, and rejection; to become more aware of those who are sick, imprisoned, on death row, or refugees. And once each month we promise to decide together to make a gift of time, food, or money to help ease the burdens of others.

- We further promise to take a moment each week to decide how much money to give to our parish through the offertory collection at Sunday Mass. We'll do this together as a household and have the offering come from everyone.

- At least once each week, as a household, we promise to do at least one thing to improve the care of the earth on which we live. (This might include recycling, picking up trash, going for a hike, or caring for a garden.)

- We promise to be present and active in the Sunday assembly each week, or as often as possible for us. And after Mass, to continue to observe Sunday as a day off from regular life, to postpone shopping and work as much as possible and try to do something together as a household, such as a meal which extends the celebration of the Mass into the rest of daily life.

- We promise to help each other memorize certain prayers and understand what they mean, and to learn about what it means to follow Christ in his Way.

- We promise to encourage each other to pray daily, and to provide means within our household to make that possible, such as prayer books, sacred spaces, occasional quiet times, and signs of our faith. We promise every night before bed to offer one another a simple blessing: "Good night. God bless you. I love you."

• As time allows us to, we promise to also volunteer time for parish programs, or for other needs of the neighborhood or community.

Both sides now. Whole community catechesis provides us a chance to "start over" on new ground in how we provide catechesis. The new ground is that, no matter what, catechesis is always done on a 50-50 Plan, household and parish. It's never the duty of just one or the other.

The benefits are clear. Parishes that have adopted this approach find that everyone has more of a sense that religious education and formation is their responsibility, whether they're parents, grandparents, neighbors, or parish staff members. Households are affirmed in living a more explicitly Christian life, and parishes are enriched as adults naturally seek more formation for themselves. It's a practical way to implement whole community catechesis.

Here's what one parent recently told me about this:

> When my two kids came home from CCD class and told me
> that everyone had to sign up for this 50-50 deal, I said, "No
> way. That's what we pay them to do down at the church."
> Looking back now, I'm not sure where I even got that idea.
> Obviously I've changed my mind after trying it.
>
> Molly [my wife] and I went down to sign up the next week
> because, you know, we wanted our kids to know about the
> church and all. So they showed us this fancy list of things the
> parish would do. But then [the volunteer doing this at their
> parish] turned the page and showed us what we could do. The
> idea of what 50-50 means started to hit home. We looked
> over that list together and then I looked up at [the volunteer]
> and said, "You mean to tell me that by recycling our trash and
> teaching our kids about that, I'm doing part of my 50%?"
>
> "Yep," she said. Suddenly it dawned on me. We were already
> doing a lot of what we had to, we just weren't connecting it to
> our faith. So we signed up for five or six things and went home.
> The next Sunday when we had our first dinner under this deal, I
> must say, it felt pretty good. Our family was together and it was
> Sunday and it sort of felt like, I don't know, like a really good
> thing for us to be doing. And that night, for the first time ever, I
> sat with [my son] and we had the TV off and we talked about
> what it was like when his grandmother died. He actually had lots
> of questions. I could see how this fit into his understanding of
> religion. I felt much closer to him than I had for a long time.
>
> It's funny. We live in the same house but we needed this to
> bring us together.

How to do this. Here are some features of using the 50-50 Plan.

- It's an annual agreement. During late summer and early fall, each
  household of the parish that wants to participate, whether or not
  they have children, recommits itself to this arrangement. This
  replaces what was "religious education enrollment" (or whatever it
  was called in your parish). It may also replace any sort of stewardship pledge card the parish may have used. Even time and talent

commitments can be rolled into this one process of inviting members of the parish to a 50-50 Plan between themselves and the parish community.

- The list of what the parish promises should be drawn up with the input of the various ministries of the parish, including the pastoral council if appropriate. Certainly, the pastor must approve whatever promises the parish makes. A caution: don't make this list too long! The focus should be on the main points of parish life: the Sunday assembly, catechesis assemblies, and pastoral care.

- The list of what households of the parish are invited to commit to may also have the input of various leaders (such as financial leaders if a stewardship pledge is part of it, or others if time and talent are included). A big caution here: be sure the focus remains on the household needs, not the needs of the parish community. Remember, the goal of parish life is better household life, not the other way around.

- All households of the parish are invited to enroll in the 50-50 Plan. Since whole community catechesis is for everyone, whether or not they have children or anyone in the catechesis assemblies does not matter. School families are involved, too. The pastor and staff are involved. Every member of the parish is invited to a 50-50 partnership with the parish community.

- The 50-50 Plan works best as a written covenant, drawn up during a personal conversation with volunteers or staff members or the pastor. The volunteers who do this should have a naturally pastoral approach to people. Often older members of the parish have the seasoning and wisdom and grace to enter into this rather personal conversation with a household. See appendix two for a sample covenant.

- These annual conversations help keep the households of the parish focused; a time to invite folks to the catechesis assemblies, answer their questions, and then exchange promises—a covenant!

- These annual household conversations are also a time for the volunteers or staff of the parish to listen to what people are asking about. Too much time? Here's what one pastor told me about this.

The first time this was presented to me in a staff meeting by [his parish director] I said to myself, "She can talk all day if she wants but I'll never agree to this because it would just take too much time." We're a busy parish. We have meetings and schedules and lots of things going on everyday. I just didn't think that sitting down with the members of each household—even if we could get them to do this with us—was worth the time!

But [the director in his parish] talked me into it! She had her homework done and she reminded me to read Canon Law, of all things! After the meeting I went and looked up the canon she cited, Canon 529 I think it was. I was quite surprised by what I found there.

[Editor's note: Here, in part, is what canon 529 says: "In order to fulfill his office in earnest, the pastor should strive to come to know the faithful who have been entrusted to his care; therefore, he is to visit families, sharing the cares, worries, and especially the griefs of the faithful, strengthening them in the Lord. He is to make a special effort to seek out the poor, the afflicted, the lonely, those exiled from their own land, and similarly those weighed down with special difficulties. . ."]

I agreed to try her plan, reluctantly.

We decided to ask some good, solid parish members to help us do this. We got them and ourselves all together in a room one evening and talked through how to approach these households. We agreed to listen as much as we talked. And this was going to be a lot of work: we have more than 900 households all together!

Well, it only took three or four household meetings for me to realize that this wasn't a waste of time at all. This wasn't extra work for me. Rather, it was the most important work I could be doing.

Here's the big thing I learned doing this work. We've had two or three generations now since the 1960s when that old European immigrant American Catholic subculture fell apart, as Andrew Greeley puts it. People are real confused about what the church teaches, about how welcome they actually are despite the irregularities in their marriages and the blending in their families. People genuinely want to live their faith—they just need a little help.

This has changed the way I preach. I used to preach about the church. Now I preach about everyday life where the church lives! These household 50-50 deals are the best parish renewal we've ever had!

A note of caution. What is a household? In today's culture, it can be difficult and harmful to use family life as the only example of divine life. There simply aren't that many families today in which there are two Catholic parents, both in good standing with the church, both living at home, and both raising the children. Without arguing whether that's a good or bad thing, let's agree that it's the real situation in which many people live. If we go on assuming that this is the family setting for most of the kids or adults in our parishes, we'll blindside ourselves.

Here's what one catechist told me in a focus group this year when I asked for evaluations of how it's going in their classrooms:

OK, I teach sixth grade. I have 17 youngsters and we're studying the Bible. First of all, the textbook has too much material in it. We do our best to cover what we can but it's too much. And secondly, it (the text) keeps instructing us to use examples from family life to illustrate what God is like. And every week there are these materials I'm supposed to send home, asking them to read the Bible together as a family!

Well, of my 17 kids, only 5 live in homes where there are two Catholic parents. Two of my students don't even live with their parents. Ten of them are in blended families! Almost all of them live with people of other faiths. And one of them has two mommies! It's the modern world, for Pete's sake. When are we gonna catch on?

Step Two: Learning to listen

There is a method for learning to listen within a parish that will help make the shift to a household-centered parish more possible. In this process, parish leaders spend more time listening and less time on the details of parish life. Echoing Canon 529 (cited above) this process allows the pastor and his key leaders and staff to spend time in a non-judgmental listening posture, hearing about the cares and concerns of those under their pastoral care.

Again, this is a shift in the framework within which we've viewed parish life. We've tended to see members of the parish with a duty to help the parish. But under the rubric of whole community catechesis, it is the duty of parish leaders to assist in revealing the reign of God in the everyday life and households of the parishioners.

See appendix three for a detailed description of this listening process. And see appendix four to read the outcome of a focus group of typical Catholics, talking about what they have on their minds these days.

Step Three: Christian homemaking

Homemaking is an ancient human activity. It's far more than providing food, firewood, and other essentials. It involves creating a particular atmosphere within a house, employing those elements that bring about a sense of belonging, welcoming, and love. Even in homes where poverty dominates the economics of the family, such an atmosphere can be created. It doesn't take a lot of money to make a home. It takes heart, and especially a Christian heart fired by the grace of Christ. Money can, in fact, be an obstacle, as Jesus himself observed many times.

Here are some of the elements, which when taken together, help make a home.

- Making time for each other, even when you're busy. Reorganize your schedule to make more time for your home life.

- Sharing laughter over the small things, like accidental ways of saying things or a funny thought you had today.

- Knowing when you're wrong or have made a mistake—and letting that fit into life for you. It really isn't necessary to point out every mistake someone living in your household makes. For Pete's sake, lighten up!

- Freely and voluntarily giving each other affirmation and support, looking for ways to compliment one another. Don't let a single meal go by without a compliment to the cook. And be full of thanks to each other for helping make your house a real home.

- Giving each other help in times of trouble—when there's addiction, depression, illness, or relationship loss—or when the money runs out and you don't have all your shopping done. Or when a childhood memory returns to haunt you, or when you hurt each other. There's nothing like forgiveness to deepen love within a household.

- Sharing meals together, especially supper—planning the menu, shopping, cooking, setting the table, cleaning up...but mainly, lingering over the meal, chatting, and allowing each other space to breathe. There's just nothing like home cooking. It's a lost art but it can be reclaimed. The supper meal can be that moment around which the entire day is organized. It's the summit of the day, the hour to which everything in the day points. There is no experience in life more important than having supper together, which is why Jesus chose to leave us with a meal rather than a textbook, a moral code, or a theology system.

- Sharing playtime, which might include things like TV shows, movies, games, or just sitting quietly in the same room, reading the Sunday paper. Stop at lawn sales, go to fairs, don't miss the doughnuts and coffee after Mass on Sunday morning.

- Decorating your house a little. It doesn't have to be fancy or expensive, but it should be really what you like. Keep the house clean, as clean as you can because it just makes the home more welcoming. And add little personal touches to it: a photo here, a favorite gift there. These displays help others see into your own heart. And it's the heart of your home that's important anyway.

- Appreciating beauty, which only sounds expensive. Many people live without noticing the beauty all around them, but beauty is one of the surest ways to be near to God.

- Listening to music. Music sends us back into the memories of the past while creating its own memories for the future. It's as close as your radio. When sitting down to supper, let music help create the atmosphere of elegance. There's nothing wrong with a little elegance.

- Enjoying smells in a house—of bread baking, cookies, the barbecue grill, garlic. One of the most important side benefits to home cooking is the smells it provides. Smells are what help make a house homey. They tell guests how welcome they are. And they jog the memory of love.

- Teaching manners, hospitality, graciousness. Again, sharing supper every evening is full of benefits. One of them is that it gives us a chance to treat each other like royalty. Learning to be hospitable to each other and to guests is one of the most important traits of a person following the Way of Christ.

- Leaving love notes for one another, or notes of support and affirmation.

- Learning to be "the big one." Sharing life in a household can be trying, even when love is abundant. Sometimes there will be conflict. Sometimes there will be one piece of cake too few. These are times when we learn the mysterious teachings of Jesus firsthand. There's a certain experience of nurturing one's inner space, one's soul, by taking the last seat, by giving twice as much as is asked, by forgiving seventy-times-seven times.

- Talking about one's faith. The events of the day, the supper no matter how simple, and even our very breath—these are all gifts. Only when you are making home can you see them that way. And now and then, talking about how God's hand provides and guides is the only true way to understand any of the arcane dogmas of the church. No theological system, with all its books and doctrines, can match what one walk in the woods as a household can tell us about God.

Teach about homemaking. The finest form of Christian adult formation is that which coaches, teaches, and shows by example how to "make home." Like making love in a marriage, making home is essential to the growth of faith. Read back over the church's own docu-

ments (which are quoted just above) and read back over that list of elements that go into "making home." There are many ways for the parish community to foster homemaking. Without it, everything else we do may be in vain.

Why? Because faith is not lived at the parish. The parish itself is not really the goal of the Gospel. Faith is lived at home. It's also learned at home, as the church's own documents repeatedly point out. So, rather than more classes on church doctrine, practices, and traditions, why not offer classes on homemaking instead? Why not help people who live alone connect for meals and parties, rather than parish meetings? Why not distribute recipes for simple but good meals, rather than fliers on liturgical seasons? Why not have cooking classes, or teach about how to be a host or a guest? Why not raise money from those who are financially well off to help others have enough money to afford shared meals?

What's the key to "making home?" Have supper together. Really. It's that simple.

A few years ago we attended the funeral of a friend who had died from the terrible diseases associated with AIDS. The family had been members of a small Unitarian church, which is where the memorial service was held. His cremated ashes stood near by.

After some singing and the reading of a few of his best-loved poems, a small orchestra played an aria from one of our friend's favorite operas. And then his life partner, another gentleman, rose to address us.

"I've learned a lot about life by going through Fred's death," he told us. "I've learned that both our families love us profoundly. I've learned that our friends will stand with us no matter what. I've learned the names of diseases I hope never to hear again: Pneumasistis carnini pneumonia, Kaposi's sarcoma. I've learned about medical procedures designed in hell that they used to try to keep Fred alive."

Then he paused as if to eye us for just a minute or two.

"But the biggest lesson I take away from all this," he said, "is that I've learned to dust less—and use the china more! Now he's dead and it's too late. Our china is sitting on the shelf, unchipped."

Unchipped china, indeed! How many of us will go to our graves with china we never used?! I say, take that china off the shelf and use it! Pause at the end of your day, even if you're a little tired, and share a meal with others. Sit down to a table, set as if for guests, even when you are only two or three or four people and you all live in the same house. Make supper the center point of your day.

Why? You ask. Because Jesus did. It's inescapable in the Gospels, no matter which one you read. In Luke alone, there are ten great meals, in the context of which Jesus carried out his ministry.

Everyday dining. And yes, we're talking here about everyday meals.

Not easy. In order to do this, you will have to reorganize your whole life, I know. Depending on your work schedule, choose a meal that will be the center point of your household's life. This means you may have to put other activities on hold. Turn off the television. Come home early from work. Have fewer evening activities, including parish activities.

The beauty of having supper together every day is that your whole household gets involved. People start asking, "What's for dinner?" early in the day. Or they want to invite a friend on Thursday. Or they decide to tape a TV show for watching later. This isn't where mom cooks, everybody eats, and mom cleans up. This is where everybody helps with every part of the meal.

Recently some neighbors stopped to see me. They have three children, all in their high school years. But the problem was that they were out of touch with their kids. They didn't even know who all their kids' friends were. They wanted to talk about some serious stuff: sex, money, careers, family history, but they didn't know how. Did I have any suggestions for them?

So I suggested they start having dinner every evening. "Set the table," I told them. "Use the good dishes. Light a candle. Put on some music. Turn off the TV. And cook together. Be around the kitchen. The smells and sounds will at least make them curious.

"Invite them," I advised, "but don't require them to eat with you. But do eat yourselves. Sit down, share the meal, chat together, and linger for a while afterward. Just see what happens."

A month later I saw these neighbors again. "You won't believe it," she said. "By the end of the second week of having supper like this, all three kids were at the table, and were asking to invite their friends, too. Now they take a turn at the cooking. We've never shopped for so many groceries in our life! And we just love it!"

And within a few months, this family was talking again. About almost everything. There was a new sense of "daily expectation" in the house. Their meals were simple; they aren't well off. But their meals were shared—and that's the key.

If you cook it, they will come. This may sound too simple, but when you cook and dine with others on a regular basis, reconciliation happens naturally. You simply cannot eat at table with people with whom you're on the outs. And when you dine together, a sense of agape (the early Christian love feast) emerges very quickly. You start to get the sense that having supper together is romantic—and it is! And you get the sense that some large non-verbal communication of love is going on that is not possible in any other context.

It can't be hit or miss dining. It must be daily, or as often as possible. Why? Because it has to be something that everyone in the household can count on. They're going to bring themselves to this, not just their appetites. Building it into the structures of how you live together is vital.

And here's another thing. Having supper in the evening at home creates a natural sense of liturgy. It's liturgical, even though not fully public. There is a table, with linens, candles, and certain vessels used in the meal. There is the shared food, the bread broken. There is wine to pour, a toast to make, lives to celebrate every single day. It takes on a liturgical air after a while.

> The other night at our table, we were feeling just a little rushed. I don't remember why. But finally, the lights were turned down, the music was on, and we were sitting. Without thinking I picked up my fork to start eating. But I was reminded that we had not observed our opening rite, the toast.
>
> Every evening we toast the people or events or notable happenings of the day. At first, it was just a lovely thing to do. Now it is the opening rite at every meal. We don't start without it. That's how liturgical tradition unfolds. For some people, this might be an opening prayer (another way of observing those notable happenings). For others, it might be the lighting of the candles, or the pouring of the wine.
>
> The important thing is having supper together as often as possible.

Let me repeat that. The most important Christian activity of the members of any parish is not the parish council meeting, it's not the choir practice, not catechesis. It's having supper in their homes together. Organize the parish so as to make room for that. Teach about it. Encourage it. And go home yourself to supper with friends, family, or loved ones.

It's also possible to add meals to present programs. For example, why not invite the parish grandparents to serve meals in the school hot lunch program? At the moment, most lunch hours in schools are eat-and-run events. But what would happen if we slowed them down and made them into something much more than that? Eating together is such an important part of community life. Why not make it more of a teaching moment in our parish schools?

As you'll see in chapter six, frameworks other than the schoolhouse model for providing catechesis make it possible to include sharing food as a part of every catechetical assembly or gathering, all week long!

Summary

So far we have proposed that (1) the Sunday assembly be the font from which the whole community draws catechesis. (2) By being made to feel welcome, even (or especially!) if they live in irregular household situations, all community members gather to share in that assembly. (3) Drawing from the homily there, all parish groups and classes, and all parish households are invited over and over and over again to share their faith with each other. And (4) all of this is situated in a deeper appreciation for being baptized, for living the paschal mystery in one's own life, dying in Christ and experiencing the wonderful sense of resurrection to which that leads for us humans. In chapter four we proposed that Christ be made more the center of all catechesis. In this we said that (1) turning our hearts to Christ, over and over again throughout our lives, precedes learning about our faith. (2) We turn our hearts to Christ by (a) sharing our faith, no matter how new or weak, with others, (b) hearing the witness of those who know Christ, (c) celebrating the sacraments with the rest of the church, and (d) meeting Christ in the poor and rejected of our society and world.

In chapter five, we added another dimension: the development of the household as a more vital place in which the faith is lived and shared. We offered three ideas for making whole community catechesis more of a reality. (1) Invite all the households of the parish to participate in catechesis on a 50-50 basis. (2) Implement a process within the parish that enables parish leaders to listen to and really hear the pastoral concerns of the members. (3) Teach, affirm, encourage, and make time for Christian homemaking within the parish, especially meals.

From time to time in this manual, we've been pausing just to realize what a very different framework emerges as the various planks of whole community catechesis are put in place. This framework leans heavily on the everyday life and experience of the members of the parish. It asks the staff and leaders of the parish to become a real resource for the people.

New frameworks take some getting used to. But let's hasten on to what are perhaps the most concrete changes proposed by whole community catechesis.

6

Catechesis Assemblies and Other Fine Ideas

*"Hope for renewing an intergenerational vision and nurturing intergenerational learning is not beyond our reach.
We are, by nature, intergenerational."*

Steven Ellair
Consultant for Elementary Catechesis, Archdiocese of Los Angeles

Catechesis can be fun!

Our goal is to make the experience of catechesis enjoyable, to make it a magnet for people young and old. The present framework within which catechesis is provided fights a little against the idea of having fun. Classroom settings mean order and discipline and a general sense that the student should be quiet and listen to the teacher.

Whole community catechesis, however, suggests that other formats for the classroom sessions might be possible.

Catechesis assemblies

What if we gathered several of those small classroom groups into one larger group? They could sit at round tables in an assembly hall (cafeteria, gym, large meeting room, KC hall, or church basement). Their classroom catechists could sit there with them, working all at once in the same room. Then a lead or master catechist could preside over all this. In such a setting, the use of media could more easily be increased. Storytelling could be provided to the whole group by trained storytellers. A dynamic back-and-forth process could occur, the lead catechist spinning out a story, then tossing it back to the table catechists to process in the small groups.

The lead catechists would be people who truly have the gift for teaching, those who can hold and move an audience of learners of all ages. Such folks exist but often do not volunteer in the present programs because they aren't ready to work in the classroom setting. Meanwhile, many who do come forward now as catechists really have the gift of facilitation. These persons can help a group move through a process or activity or discussion, even if they can't teach it very well.

This larger setting could also be a place where more planning and better quality could go into liturgical prayer. The sessions could run longer than fifty-five minutes on Wednesday evening. They could run for ninety minutes or two hours, the typical length of a movie, for example. They could open with singing and liturgical prayer, take 15 minutes to talk about the Question of the Week in small groups, move into a focusing activity for that night's topic with media or a story, then shift gears into a more content-oriented period. There could be a break after an hour or so, for food and beverages, then the final part of the evening could be activity oriented: plays, artwork, a guest speaker, or whatever.

Parents, grandparents, or general parishioners could be invited to attend these because, unlike the classroom, such an assembly would feel more open, more welcoming to guests. Guests in a classroom are noticed and often feel out of place. But in these assemblies, they seem a natural part of the flow. Volunteer catechists would be easier to recruit because they'd be under less pressure to organize and run a full class session themselves. And most importantly, the participants would feel happier about their experience because it would seem so much more like church and so much less like school.

We could mix grade levels for these assemblies, but we would need to be certain that we continue to provide a comprehensive presentation of the faith at each grade level, as the U.S. bishops have asked us to do.

Of course, our secret plan here is to have more adults participate by shifting to these catechesis assemblies for the children's program.

This is the beginning point for drawing in the whole rest of the community. To simply stop offering a children's program would be too radical a move in most places. It would cause confusion, anger, and upset. But gradually shifting from a children's-only program into one in which the whole community can participate will work. All it takes is leadership and heart.

Many parishes are already working with some form of these assemblies. Many others are on the brink of making this shift. Appendix six provides a table showing this in detail. And see appendix seven for an outline on shaping these assemblies.

And if these assemblies work for children's programs, then why not use them throughout the parish? Wouldn't they be a wonderful context in which to provide preparation for celebrating the sacraments, for example? Imagine the energy and enthusiasm you could generate for Eucharist! What a great context in which to help couples prepare for marriage, or to strengthen an existing marriage! Would this not be a fantastic setting in which to help young couples prepare for the baptism of their newborn children? We can rethink all the catechetical ministries of the parish with an eye to

• providing a more liturgical setting for them all

• beginning each with faith-sharing to encourage deeper conversion to the Lord

• bringing together folks of varying ages and backgrounds to share the experiences

• making these events exciting by use of music, media, faith-sharing, eating and drinking, storytelling and other forms of communication

• letting those with the gift of teaching lead and those with the gift of facilitating facilitate.

Such an approach could be used effectively for

• leadership training

• ministry training for pastoral care or liturgy

• spirituality workshops and growth opportunities

• Bible studies

- sacramental preparation
- the movement for justice and peace.

New frameworks mean new tasks.
Change is never easy and changing one's thinking is the most difficult. But as Thoreau pointed out, the antecedent of every action is a
thought. And right now, our parish workers are busy. They don't have
a lot of free time to rethink what they're doing and reorganize. Here's
what one parish director told me recently:

> If the message light on my office phone is blinking at 4:30 on
> the afternoon before evening religious ed classes, I know that
> one of my volunteers is not going to make it tonight. That
> means I'm going to have to find a substitute teacher for that
> class fast! Just holding all this together week in and week out
> is a major effort. So when the pastor or the diocesan office or,
> God forbid, one of the publishers, comes along with a work-
> shop advising me to change something major in my program,
> I nod, agree with everything they say, and then go home and
> basically do what I did last week: I keep 120 volunteers, 730
> kids, and who-knows-how-many parents happy. Not much
> changes. I mean, I agree we need to change this system, but
> who's going to do it?

As this parish religious ed director suggests, we may not be fully
comfortable with our current way of providing religious education.
But we are getting through each week under the present system: we
know what textbooks we need, what spaces should be reserved in
the parish buildings, what the schedule for the year will look like,
what sort of staff and volunteer workers we'll need, and how to write
a budget to cover all this.

A community effort. So the task of reforming catechesis does not
belong only to parish directors and catechists. It truly belongs to the
whole community. What if a parish task force were established to
plan such a shift? What if a single leader were identified, someone
who could articulate this vision and solve problems and make sure
that the people involved presently were not hurt by this shift?

In this or similar formats. Some form of assembly seems like the right way to go in searching for a better framework within which to effectively share the faith. These assemblies may organize all the parents in one group and the youngsters in another. They may involve everyone for a half hour, then continue with smaller groups for the rest of the evening, ending with food and beverages. However they're organized, catechesis assemblies seem like a suitable format for whole community catechesis.

In one parish where catechesis assemblies, similar to what I've described above, are in use, the director recently wrote this:

> The "students" (I hesitate to call them students any longer because they really aren't in school anymore) sat at round tables accompanied by as many of their catechists and parents as possible. Parents readily came forward to be present but so did others in the parish, many of them former classroom catechists that I used to recruit the hard way! Within two or three weeks of this new approach, as word got out that it was much safer for them than those classrooms had been, some parents began attending every week. They were invited and even encouraged to do so by the program. So any given table had several students, accompanied by several adults. We retained the use of our textbook series. It actually served us better in this new format than it had in the old. The lead catechists and I planned each assembly very carefully, balancing faith-sharing, storytelling, liturgy, quiet time, sharing at the tables, and instruction right out of the book.
>
> We loved our volunteer catechists! Boy did they have heart! But they themselves felt under-prepared for their roles. They worked so hard to keep order and to do an adequate job in those classrooms. When we asked them about it, they told us they felt relieved that their role in preparing and leading the session would be reduced.
>
> We employed "lead catechists" who were paid a small stipend, had the gift of teaching, and were very well prepared each week. These lead catechists were drawn from the ranks of

the volunteers—the cream of that crop, as it were. This person led the catechetical process for the entire room, using a microphone. I can't emphasize enough how important the gift of teaching is to this process. It is one of the biggest changes we experienced. It simply hadn't occurred to us that many of our well-meaning volunteers did not have that gift. They had big hearts, free time, and kids in the program themselves, but sometimes not the gift of teaching. But as gifted teachers came to the surface in the parish, the Spirit was unleashed here! Wow! Those people can really hold a crowd and help them learn!

The lead catechists called for times of faith-sharing, times of learning the doctrine, and activities to make it all real. They mixed excellent catechesis with fine group liturgical prayer and music. They used well-prepared media mixed with quiet times of prayer with the lights turned low. It was solid catechesis with excellent pedagogy. I swear, in the end, everyone knew more of the catechism and not less!

And those catechists and parents at each table had a ball! By the fourth week of this, we had many more adults than we needed, but it didn't matter because everyone was learning from each other! It really was quite amazing.

And here is the miracle of it: suddenly and overnight, religious education was no longer dreaded by parents, kids, or catechists. Instead, it was an exciting weekly event in the parish to which everyone was invited and to which most looked forward. It is slowly becoming what its name says: whole community catechesis. Not to mention that recruiting volunteers for every classroom was no longer needed, to everyone's delight!

Many options

There are many options for organizing catechesis assemblies across generational lines. The pattern of these assemblies will vary in every parish. There is no one plan. And the plan followed in one parish may vary from year to year. In all of these cases, it's possible to organize a large group event with pizzazz and energy, an event to which people young and old will look forward. It's possible to make every assembly a real event in the life of the parish, to become a magnet! Parishes now using this approach find they don't have room for everyone who wants to be part of it! What a great problem to have! And the result is that the Sunday assembly is more potent, too! Contributions to the parish rise! Most importantly, evangelization occurs every single day as members of the parish become better homemakers, and others experience the love and hospitality of those homes!

All doctrinal bases are covered

And beyond that, the important doctrine, tradition, and rites of the church are passed on by both the lead catechist and the table cate-chists. In fact, more solid doctrine, tradition, and ritual knowledge is shared than ever occurred in those old classrooms! And it's shared in a context that looks like the whole church: an assembly of folks from many backgrounds and all ages.

Here is what Steven Ellair, Consultant for Elementary Catechesis in the Archdiocese of Los Angeles, noted about this:

> Our "school-mode" applications of religious education also lead to more cognitively focused "classrooms." This approach can lead to a de-emphasis on the affective and behavioral dimensions of learning, and produce children who can recite prayers and church doctrine, but who have little or no com-mitment to Church.... Intergenerational learning is by nature experiential and relational.

And here's what John Roberto of the Center for Ministry Development noted in the introduction to his "Generations of Faith," a fine intergenerational model for catechesis:

> The current programmatic and age-specific approach to child-hood and adolescent faith formation, that has characterized the efforts of so many parishes over the past thirty years, is simply not adequate. It may be one of the models of faith for-mation in a parish, but it cannot be the only model. It is time to broaden our vision and our practice.

Still at the parish. In Pope John Paul II's teachings the parish remains the place where catechesis should occur, in addition to the home. Whole community catechesis assigns tremendous responsibility to the household of the learner. But it remains a part of shared parish life, just as the Sunday assembly does. Here's what the pope has to say about this, noted in *Catechesi Tradendae*, his teaching on catechesis published in 1979:

Catechesis always has been and always will be a work for which the whole Church must feel responsible and wish to be responsible.

The summary table found in appendix six emphasizes the important new language with which we describe this new framework for providing catechesis. The new language is vitally important! It will help shape and deliver the new outcomes we seek: lifelong learning and growing, lifelong faith-sharing, lifelong shared meals, and a shared love for the poor.

Summary

So far we have proposed that (1) the Sunday assembly be the font from which the whole community draws catechesis. (2) By being made to feel welcome, even (or especially!) if they live in irregular household situations, all community members gather to share in that assembly. (3) Drawing from the homily there, all parish groups and classes, and all parish households are invited over and over and over again to share their faith with each other. And (4) all of this is situated in a deeper appreciation for being baptized, for living the paschal mystery in one's own life, dying in Christ and experiencing the wonderful sense of resurrection to which that leads for us humans.

In chapter four we proposed that Christ be made more the center of all catechesis. In this we said that (1) turning our hearts to Christ, over and over again throughout our lives, precedes learning about our faith. (2) We turn our hearts to Christ by (a) sharing our faith, no matter how new or weak, with others, (b) hearing the witness of those who know Christ, (c) celebrating the sacraments with the rest of the Church, and (d) meeting Christ in the poor and rejected of our society and world.

In chapter five, we added another dimension: the development of the household as a more vital place in which the faith is lived and shared. We offered three ideas to make whole community catechesis more a reality. (1) Invite all the households of the parish to participate in catechesis on a 50-50 basis. (2) Implement a process within the parish by which it becomes more possible to listen to and really hear the pastoral concerns of the members. (3) Teach, affirm, encourage, and make time for Christian homemaking within the parish, especially meals.

In chapter six we proposed a new framework within which to offer catechetical instruction for children and adults, and perhaps even for all the various catechetical moments that occur within parish life. This chapter occurs last in the succession of ideas being presented in this manual because it's certainly possible to implement everything leading up to this suggestion while maintaining the schoolhouse framework for religious instruction. At first many parishes may feel very uncomfortable giving up the schoolhouse model. It's so well-known and recognizable and has served us for so long that changing it might seem too daunting a task.

Why not try a pilot with one group, or within one dimension of your current program, as a way to get started? Why not talk this over with your catechists and see what they think might be possible? Regardless what you decide about catechesis assemblies, however, you can still proceed with all the other aspects of whole community catechesis.

Appendix 1
The Question of the Week

Ideally the parish staff will prepare a one-page sheet for everyone in the parish to use throughout the week (whether you decide to share the readings for the following weekend, or to reflect on the homily and readings of the previous weekend). Here's what that one-page sheet might look like:

Faith-sharing Guide for St. Somebody's Parish (date)

The Call to Prayer

Leader: My friends, let's pause a moment here in the midst of all our activity to prepare ourselves to spend a few moments of prayer with God and each other.

The Word of God

Leader: The Lord be with you!

All: And also with you!

Leader: +A reading from the holy Gospel according to

_____.

All: Glory to you, O Lord!

(the Gospel reading or a part thereof.)

Leader: The Gospel of the Lord.

All: Praise to you, Lord Jesus Christ!

The Faith-sharing

Leader: This week the parish is sharing faith based on this question: (present the Question of the Week and allow time for sharing.)

At the end of the sharing period, invite folks to pray in one of the following ways:

The Lord's Prayer out loud together

Spontaneous prayers

A moment of silent prayer

Sing along with a recorded hymn

Sample questions of the week:

When the Gospel recounts the teachings of Christ (such as at the Beatitudes, or various of Christ's instructions to his followers)

"Which one of these Beatitudes did you most notice when you heard them read again today? And how will you make that Beatitude more a part of your everyday life?"

When the Gospel repeats a parable of Jesus, or tells a story of healing or forgiveness:

"How do you picture yourself in this story? How have you experienced Christ touching your life as he did these people's lives?"

When the Gospel tells about an incident in Jesus' life where he encountered people around him in his culture, such as church leaders, passersby, or others:

"When you think back over the past three or four days, how have you experienced Christ present around you? When might you have experienced his absence?"

For the School:

A. Develop a "Question of the Week" drawn from the Sunday readings.

It should be a question that leads to "theological reflection" without being too theological itself. Not a "yes" or "no" question, but one that draws the user deeper into the Gospel.

A question that asks for a *personal* response. It's not a discussion *about* the faith but a sharing of one's own faith and belief.

One that is age-appropriate—but still has teeth!

B. Within the school, someone "delivers" this Question each week by sharing about it him or herself as part of a school prayer service.

This requires that a special prayer service be held each week, either as an assembly or in each classroom. First thing Monday morning is best! By doing this, you "teach" the young how important it is to share faith.

Base the prayer service on the readings for either the previous or the upcoming Sunday. Let the Gospel reading shape the Question of the Week.

C. Repeat the Question of the Week in the school bulletin, send it home, use it in the faculty meeting and in every class. Invite the rest of the parish to join you by sharing it with other staff members. In the classrooms:

- Monday: Hold the school assembly for prayer.
- Tuesday: Re-read the Gospel at the start of the day; ask each student to *share faith* in a small group setting based on the Question. Invite two or three students to share with the large group. Rotate these sharers until everyone has shared with the large group, and then start over!
- Wednesday: Re-read the Gospel again! Invite the students to decide on one way this Gospel invites them to change *how they live*. Work in small groups for this. Ask each small group to "report" to the large group. You might ask them to illustrate their discussion somehow.
- Thursday: Re-read the Gospel yet again! Ask students to work in small groups to *compose a prayer* based on this Gospel reading.
- Friday: Hold a classroom prayer service in which the prayers of the students form the basis of the prayer.

Appendix 2
Sample 50-50 Contract

St. Somebody's Parish

50-50 Partnership Agreement

The household of
Names:
Address:
Phone:
E-mail:

1) We promise to offer one another more love in our household, through the exchange of love notes, gifts, and other signs of affection. We'll try to pay more attention to one another, caring for each other, and offering each other both privacy and companionship.

2) At least once a month, we'll spend time (with the TV off) compiling a family scrapbook and photo album containing bits and pieces from the people and events of our household.

3) We promise to share one significant household meal each week, adding a bit of romance to our table (candlelight, wine, and flowers). We'll try to cook together, linger for a while at the table, and clean up together.

4) If there's a quarrel within our household, we'll work for reconciliation which is explicit and expressed in words such as "I am sorry" and "I forgive you."

5) We promise to become more conscious of those people in our family, neighborhood, parish, or wider society whom we dislike. We promise to gossip less and affirm more.

6) We promise to give some of our money for the needs of the parish

and the care of the poor. At this point, we promise to give _____ during this year. We will take a moment each week to decide together how much money we can afford to give to other needs.

7) At least once each week, as a household, we promise to do at least one thing to improve the care of the earth on which we live. This might include recycling, picking up trash, going for a hike, or caring for a garden.

8) We promise to be present and active in the Sunday assembly each week, or as often as possible for us. After Mass, we'll continue to observe Sunday as a "day off" from regular life. We'll postpone shopping and work as much as possible and try to do something together as a household, such as a meal, which extends the celebration of the Mass into the rest of our lives.

9) We'll help each other memorize certain prayers and lists, and understand what they mean. We'll encourage each other to pray daily, and we'll provide means within our household to make that possible, such as prayer books, sacred spaces, occasional quiet times, and signs of our faith. Every night before bed we'll offer one another a simple blessing: "Good night. God bless you. I love you."

10) We also promise to contribute some of our free time for the needs of the parish itself. We have marked the attached sign-up sheet to show how we will do this. As time allows us to, we'll also volunteer time for parish programs, or other needs of the neighborhood or community.

On the part of the parish
We, the parish leaders of St. Somebody's parish, speaking on behalf of all, make the following promises to you as a household:

1) We promise to make the Sunday assembly the single most important focal point of parish life. We'll prepare for it carefully and help you as a household to be well disposed for it, ready to participate, and actively engaged in the rites. Each week at the assembly, we will offer you a significant question arising from the Sunday readings on which you can share as a household of faith.

2) We'll welcome you to our Sunday assembly regardless of your situation in life, whether you're married, single, widowed, divorced, remarried, in an ecumenical or interfaith marriage, gay or lesbian, or sharing a home without marriage; whether you're an immigrant or a newcomer; whether you're fully abled or handicapped, healthy or sick, old or young; whether you're struggling with your faith or firm in your commitment. We'll maintain an open door and an open heart to you, and we'll offer you a share in the grace of Christ which fills this church.

3) We'll offer you a quality religious education program and we promise to use instructional materials approved by the local bishop and faithful to the wider Catholic Christian church. We promise that the catechists who teach in the parish program will be prepared for their work, and will truly "echo the faith" in their own lives.

4) We also promise to be a resource center for your household, making available the materials that best meet your needs, including books, videos, music, and web sites.

5) From time to time, we also promise to offer evening or Saturday programs to assist you as a household in living your faith more openly and explicitly. We will assist you in following the liturgical year in your own home, especially during Advent and Lent.

6) We'll also help you as a household find ways to serve the ill, the poor, the rejected, and the suffering. If you wish, we'll train you to visit the sick, the imprisoned, the lonely, and the refugee. We'll help you become aware of the needs of the local community in which you live.

7) In general, we're here for you, to help deepen and affirm your faith and your Way of Life. We promise to assemble each Sunday to celebrate the Lord's Supper and to welcome you to join us. Beyond that, we promise to provide the resources you need to help you live within your household according to the Christian Way of Life.

Appendix 3
Listen to Your People

Parish Listening Process

A process to help determine the pastoral needs
of the community.

The "two by two" project

"The joys and hopes, the grief and anguish of the people of
our time, especially of those who are poor or afflicted, are
the joys and hopes, the grief and anguish of the followers
of Christ as well. Nothing that is genuinely human fails to
find an echo in their hearts."

Pastoral Constitution on the Church in the Modern World, #1

Overview

Through the "two by two" project, pastoral council members meet the members of the parish in their homes where people live their everyday lives. About eight times each year, council members make these home visits going out two by two to have supper or lunch with the members of that household. They share a simple meal with their hosts and over supper, they enter into a conversation about their joys and hopes, their grief and anguish. In particular, the members of the council will hear what the experience of this parish is like for average people who might not otherwise have a voice and about issues and concerns that never make most council agendas. Arrangements for this dinner are made through an official matchmaker working closely with parish leaders and the pastor.

Then, with the permission of the hosts the stories these average members of the church tell are brought back to the next council meeting. On the basis of these actual pastoral stories, pastoral planning proceeds. Pastoral planning of this sort, making an immediate response to current pastoral needs, never ends. It's the work of the parish, the work canon law gives to the pastor, and the work of the pastoral council.

Indeed, Canon 529 says this in part: "In order to fulfill his office in earnest, the pastor should strive to come to know the faithful who have been entrusted to his care; therefore, he is to visit families, sharing the cares, worries, and especially the griefs of the faithful, strengthening them in the Lord. He is to make a special effort to seek out the poor, the afflicted, the lonely, those exiled from their own land, and similarly those weighed down with special difficulties. . ."

Our presupposition is that "the faithful" to whom canon law refers is not limited to members of the parish. The church includes the parish but is bigger and more diverse than that, including God's people in a wide variety of lifestyles, households, and connections.

Our mission as followers of Jesus is not limited to developing dynamic parishes but is also directed to all people inside and outside the parish.

How did the old saying go? "Many whom the church has, God does not have, and many whom God has, the church does not have."

Getting Ready for Part 1

Preliminary work: Have the enthusiastic support and participation of the priests, pastoral staff, and council members. Rearrange pastoral council business to make time for this, letting another group or person handle most of the administrative details of the parish. Ask council members to commit themselves to about 8 extra evenings of work during the year.

The Matchmaker

Choose someone to act as a "matchmaker." This person might be a parish staff member who knows the parish well and is involved with pastoral care of souls at the present time. It's important to be in touch especially with those who might otherwise be overlooked. This matchmaker will also be able to coach the hosts in order to help them articulate their experience of the parish and the church. This person must have the trust of the council in order to make arrangements. He or she should also be available to attend some dinners where appropriate, in order to assist with preparations, conversation, and the ease of both the hosts and the guests. The matchmaker should be someone who will not take over the program and make it his or hers but will allow it to belong to the pastoral council.

The Invitation

Invite members of the parish community to host a dinner. Use the bulletin and let people come forth. Invite those who might otherwise be overlooked, especially the unchurched, those who attend Mass infrequently, ecumenical households, and those who might think they aren't welcome.

Through the matchmaker, set a time for supper in the host's home, coaching the hosts to speak honestly, forthrightly, and charitably, and coaching the guests to listen with grace, ask appropriate questions, and tell their own story in return.

The host must understand that their story will be retold to the entire pastoral council but will be treated with dignity and respect. Confidentiality, therefore, cannot be promised.

The Cost

Make a small fund available to help defray the costs of the suppers. Keep the meals simple. You might even want to suggest a simple menu, and the guests might bring a bottle of wine, a loaf of bread, or other host gift.

The Appointed Hour

At the appointed hour the guests arrive. (Everyone will be just a bit nervous.) Greetings at the door, introductions to other members of the household, maybe some appetizers in the living room before supper is served will allow everyone to feel more at home with each other.

Then to supper itself. Who will begin? Will the guests first say something about their own background briefly describing their own faith journeys? Or will the host begin, telling about their lives and offering insights into their own journeys? The guests will have been coached to help unfold the story, asking how this or that felt, letting the hosts be at ease. The guests are there to listen to these members of the church, not to preach, teach, or witness. There is no need to be defensive or apologetic.

There is simply a need to understand the everyday life experience of these people, to listen carefully to their joys and hopes, their griefs and anxieties. There is a need to hear their response to parish life, activities, and demands.

At the end of the meal, after thank yous and good-byes are said, a new chapter will open up for the parish, a new voice will have been heard, a new idea will have been raised, and in this, the voice of God calls us to new life.

Breaking Open the Word

At the very next council meeting, the guests at this meal should retell what they saw and heard at supper with God's faithful people.

What were the most vexing troubles faced in this household?

How did these people seek to live out their baptism, their own call to holiness?

What hopes did they express? What despair?

How do they view the opportunities or demands which the parish makes on them?

What help do they need in their faith journey?

What hand can be outstretched to them?

What heart opened?

What misunderstanding cleared up?

What special need met?

How can their relationship to the Lord be fostered?

The council's discussion of these events is a sacred charge because in these stories we are hearing the word of the people of God.

We break it open, just as we do the Scriptures or the tradition of the church.

In breaking it open, we want to see how God is speaking to us through the lives of these people.

If appropriate, you might invite these hosts to tell their own story to the council, or perhaps even to the whole parish the following Sunday.

The faith and life of the entire community is strengthened when these stories are told and when the path to the Lord is shared with others.

To whom should we listen?

We should not be afraid to invite the whole people of God to be heard, even those with whom we disagree. The most obvious group with which to begin might be "normal families" who are under all sorts of stress today.

Let them speak about family planning questions, about changes in their lives as they age, about the cares of their children, about their available time and money for church needs, and about how they hope to pass on their faith to their children.

But soon after, it will be clear that single parent families are also quite "normal" today.

Listen to them as well.

Let them speak of their own cares: their struggle to make ends meet, their need for support, their possible shame in being single, their loss of relationship, if any, and their ability to assist in parish life.

And then soon after these, another group will appear, those who wish to have children but do not.

Others will come forward, including gay or lesbian couples, some with children, and some without.

After them, perhaps those who have entered their last years, and those who have begun retirement.

Immigrants may come next, those who have been exiled from their own land, and those who have sought a better life for their families.

Some will be migrant workers, others will be refugees, and still others displaced for other reasons.

What about households in which illness is dominant, or injuries of any kind, and those who are living in poverty, abuse, or addiction?

There will be other households where loneliness reigns, and others who simply seem lost. Some will be seeking greater holiness, some will have given up on the church, and others will simply be stagnant. The divorced need a special ear from the church, an open and frank discussion of their situation as they consider entering a second marriage perhaps, or at least a second serious relationship. Former priests, sisters, and brothers may have their say as well, and also their spouses and partners.

There are many today who live in ecumenical households, under pressure to appear in both churches, to give time and money to both, and to rear their children in both traditions.

What a story they will have to tell us!

We should not forget to listen openly to women today, whose place in the church is the subject of much debate and who often do not feel heard by us.

How will we listen to young people who sit at table with us? They will need special care because they are not able to articulate their cares very well yet.

And those who deal daily with physical or mental abilities that are outside the norm.

Widows in our parishes have a story to tell, a story of loss, of grief, of a funeral experience with us.

And those living in "public sin," those sharing households without marriage, those remarried after divorce, gay or lesbian couples in permanent union, and others.

Another large group seeking our ear are those from a more traditional background in the church who seek the return of the "old days" of Latin, Benediction, and devotions.

Are we big enough to invite them to speak to us and to help us understand their desires?

Oh, this list could certainly go on and on. Each parish will know who to add, and who to find.

Appendix 4
What People Want to Know

From the horse's mouth. I asked a group of average Catholics in a focus group last year to identify those matters which are most important to them, to be able to live their faith on an everyday basis. Interestingly, the subject of the parish or school in their neighborhood did not even come up! That doesn't mean the parish is not important to them, or that the parish is not necessary to their faith. But the top thirty questions that arise when they stop to think about how they'll live their faith are the following in no particular order. Of course, this is not a statistically correct sample of all Catholics, but this focus group gives us some insight into what some people are asking about.

- Is divorce inevitable?
- How much is too much money for a Christian to have?
- Do I work too much?
- What is my soul like?
- Am I free now to do anything I want?
- What are the essential things I must believe to be Catholic?
- Why did my child die so young?
- What does God really want from me?
- Who will take care of me when I'm old?
- Why does sex seem to be everywhere these days?
- Can my child marry a Jew?
- Why do I worry so much about the fate of the world?
- What should I say to my neighbor who had an abortion last spring?
- Are they serious about loving beggars, lepers, and other people rejected by society?

- Does God cause earthquakes?
- Whose job is it really to feed the poor?
- When is lying wrong? (Everyone's doing it!)
- Are there still mortal sins?
- How can I balance all the demands of my life?
- Is there really a heaven?
- Why don't we allow gay people to love each other?
- Who's more Christian: democrats or republicans?
- Is the Bible literally true?
- What should I say to my gay son?
- Are babies born in the state of grace?
- Can the church help us figure out how to raise our kids?
- Should I send my mother to the nursing home or not?
- Does our dog have a soul?
- What should I do if I think my company is doing immoral things?
- Who really speaks for God these days?

Appendix 5
A Fine Method for Teaching about Baptism

A sample program

Here is a four-week unit on baptism that can be used in your catechesis assemblies. Use it as presented here, or modify it to suit your situation and culture. In this unit, those in catechesis (young and old) meet a child about to be baptized. They sew the baptismal garment as a quilt, each sewing his or her own faith into this baptism. They trim a candle. They prepare the rite. They write the baptismal promises in their own words. And when the time comes, they welcome and bless the newly baptized! And then they hold a party!

Here are some preparatory details

First, you may have to suspend for a few weeks the work outlined in your textbook series. But don't worry. You'll get back to it. The point is this: if those in catechesis don't understand and incorporate baptism in their lives, nothing else you teach will make any sense anyway.

Second, this process does not merely provide a deeper academic understanding of the theology, but offers the opportunity for a deep, interior change on the part of the learner and observer alike. It leads to real conversion. Everyone—from the family with the child to be baptized to the presiding priest or deacon—will be touched deeply.

Third, before proceeding, talk this over with your pastor and staff. If they seem reluctant, ask them to support you in one episode of the project, one four-week experiment. You cannot proceed without the support of the pastor and liturgical leaders of the parish.

Fourth, with the pastor's help and permission, find a family seeking baptism for their child, who are willing to participate in this process.

The first time you put this process into action, you may experience some reluctance on the part of folks. It's a new idea, and new ideas always take some getting used to.

Knowing ahead of time who the family will be is essential, as you will see. You can tell them that this will be a baptism like no other, and also that their child will be surrounded in a loving and rich community experience.

Note: This way of incorporating baptism into the catechesis assemblies is not perfect, especially from a liturgical point of view. As a result, in some parishes, the leaders of the liturgy may object since, in this process, the rite of baptism is celebrated outside of the Sunday assembly and within a catechesis assembly instead.

Fifth, the parish (or school) director and lead catechists prepare for the catechesis assembly by following the four-part unit given below. They work with the pastor and parish liturgical leaders.

Week One

Goal: To help those in the catechesis assembly understand baptism by participating in its preparation.

Process: In the first week, the catechesis assembly will (1) meet the child (and family) about to be baptized and learn his or her name. (2) As a group, they will then prepare a baptismal garment and (3) trim a candle for the newly baptized.

The Child: Invite the family with the child to be baptized to appear briefly during the first week of preparation. Let those in the catechesis assembly meet the child and learn his or her name. Send the family off with a blessing.

The Garment. Following the custom of many cultures, the garment will be made by the people in the catechesis assemblies. It will be a sort of "quilt" made by the participants. (Don't worry if the garment is not pure white.)

As an expression of their commitment to the newly baptized, each participant prepares a quilt square. Or, each small group works together on a single quilt square composed of the individuals' own pieces. It works well to use small pieces of cloth, one for each participant or group, on which each person draws a picture, or writes a word of Scripture or a short phrase telling what it means to them to "put on Christ like a garment." Fasten these pieces of cloth with pins to a backing cloth, to form a quilt. (Between sessions, an adult will sew this together and eliminate the pins.)

The table leaders in each small group will guide this process, working under the direction of the lead catechist.

The Song: At this same gathering, the catechesis assembly learns a short "welcoming song." They will sing this to the family and child the following week. Rehearsal is important. The song should be simple. Here are some words used in one parish for this purpose:

> We welcome you, with hearts as well as voices
> We welcome you, and all the church rejoices!
> We welcome you, as sisters and brothers,
> Come join us now in baptism: we welcome you!

The Candle: Invite the persons at each table to make and decorate one part of a large pillar candle. Provide tissue paper for each table to prepare one of the following: the newly baptized person's name; parents' or grandparents' names; baptism date; parish name; sponsors' names; symbols of baptismal commitment; symbols used in the rite of baptism.

Fasten these decorations to the pillar candle using small pins. During the following week, ask someone to attach them more permanently using a small amount of hot wax.

Presentation. After the candle and quilt are completed, allow each group to show and explain what they've done. This whole exercise takes about an hour and a half. Between this week and next, the staff and leaders should examine the garment and candle to be certain everything is secure and safe on it.

Week Two

Goal: To help those in the catechesis assembly understand that, when someone new joins the church, all the members change and grow. They are called on to welcome the newcomer, to live a deeper Christian commitment, and to help the newcomer grow in faith.

Process: All those in the catechesis assembly work together to write the baptismal promises in their own words. What do these promises mean? How are they lived out in real life? What are the challenges to living this way? (Even young children can do this exercise. It's hard to imagine anyone being ready for first Eucharist or first Reconciliation who hasn't completed an exercise like this.)

The Honorary Sponsors: Each member of the catechesis assembly becomes an "honorary sponsor" for the person about to be baptized. They each prepare a note for the newly baptized in which they state their commitment to their own baptismal promises. How will they live their lives differently in order to make the church a better place for this new member? The lead catechist can lead this process, with the table parents coaching. This experience helps participants integrate the baptismal promises in their lives.

The Song: Rehearse the welcome song again.

The Rite: At this same gathering, the catechesis assembly is introduced to the rite itself. For this, you will need to have a large tub of water in the room, as well as oil, the paschal candle, and the books of the rite. Let everyone get a little wet! It's messy (and the janitors hate it!) but it's the only way to learn. Let them rub a bit of the oil on their hands. Briefly review the rite itself. You may wish to use a video to help you with this. If possible, ask the designated presider for the rites to be present for a few minutes to help build up excitement in the catechesis assembly. You may wish to invite the family and child to be baptized as well.

The Candle and Garment: Have them ready to show everyone— explaining how they fit into the rite itself.

An Invitation: Before they leave tonight, give each member of the catechesis assembly an invitation to his or her whole extended family to attend next week. Ask everyone to "dress up" a little for the rites the following week. Mention that there will be a party with cake next week after the baptism.

Week Three:

Goal: To experience the rite of baptism.

Process: Gather everyone in the catechesis assembly hall. Rehearse the welcome song one more time. It's wonderful at this time to build a little excitement. This is a moment of celebration!

The Welcome: When the rehearsal is finished, ask everyone to wait patiently for a few minutes. The waiting is part of the experience. Meanwhile, the family of the person to be baptized arrives and is met by a host. The presider is vesting right there in the assembly hall. The baptism font is readied.

After a pause, the family knocks loudly on the door of the assembly hall. The presider says loudly, "What do you ask of the church?" The family says back loudly, through the closed door, "We want baptism for our child." The doors are then opened and the family enters to the applause of the entire catechesis assembly and its guests. The family is encircled by everyone, along with the presider, and the assembly sings the welcome song to them.

The presider completes the dialogue in the opening of the rite and then the whole assembly processes, messily, to the baptismal font, singing.

The Rite: At the font the rite is completed. It's best if the presider can memorize most of the rite so that it proceeds smoothly. What a special moment to watch as the baby is dunked, naked, into the water. And again, to see the baby—clothed in the very garment made by the assembly—lifted high and presented to the church. If possible, let some members of the catechesis assembly trace the Sign of the Cross on the newly baptized.

Afterward: Don't let the evening pass without a party to welcome the new member of the church and celebrate the moment. You really can't have a baptism like this without a sheet cake!

Week Four

Goal: To help those in the catechesis assembly remember and consolidate what they have learned (mystagogia).

Process: The catechesis assembly returns to its regular groups in the assembly hall.

The first step is to review with everyone what happened over the past three weeks. Let the catechesis assembly help with this, recalling each detail of the rite, humming the music, returning to the symbols (don't forget the sheet cake!). If the rites were videotaped, show parts of that to help everyone get back into the flow of the actual events.

The second step is to invite everyone to say aloud what touched them or moved them most, or what they remember best or most about all this. To accomplish this, you might invite them to draw a picture of what they remember most. You might want them to write a thank-you note to the family of the newly baptized. You might find other ways to help the members of the catechesis assembly express what they have experienced.

It's a very good idea to invite into this process all those in the parish who are preparing for the baptism of their child. Nothing could more adequately help them understand baptism than this celebration with the assembly. During the fourth week, this group may want to have a little extra time to talk about what the process means for them and the baby they wish to have baptized.

The winners. In this baptismal catechesis, everyone wins. The family of the newly baptized is evangelized and made to feel welcome. The entire extended family will likewise share in this welcome and hospitality. The learners and their mentor-sponsors—and indeed, their entire families—will also experience a renewed sense of what baptism means.

This process helps the whole parish grow! Later, when baptism is routinely celebrated in the Sunday assembly, everyone involved will have a much better sense of why the celebration of baptism is so important for the community.

Twice each year. Make it a rule of thumb in your community to give baptism its due importance. Find at least two opportunities each year to catechize about it by celebrating it. This is one example of how whole community catechesis leads to a deeper, more profound sense of the Catholic Christian faith throughout the parish.

Appendix 6
A Chart Showing the New Language of Catechesis Assemblies

Whole Community Catechesis: One Way to Do It!

• Using catechesis assemblies, master or lead catechists, and inviting everyone in the parish to participate.

• The catechist is one who has a vocation for this work, and has received the *gift of teaching* from the Holy Spirit.

The first and last point of reference of this catechesis will always be Jesus Christ, who is the Way, the Truth, and the Life. (*Catechism of the Catholic Church*, #1698)

Religious Education (as we do it now)		Whole Community Catechesis (as it can be done in every parish)	
in parish programs	**in schools**	**in parish programs**	**in schools**
Parish religious education "program" (pre-school through about grade 8)	Religious program or "class"	**Whole Community Catechesis,** referring to catechesis for all age groups—pre-school through adult, including those in school.	
Mainly young people within the parish	School students	Truly for young people, youth, young adults, and adults of all life situations and ages, sometimes on **an intergenerational basis.**	
An optional program for which you sign up if you wish to take part	A class in school	A **"constitutive part"** of being a parish member, just as Eucharist is constitutive or basic to being Catholic.	
Religious Ed. or CCD class	Religion class	**Catechesis assembly (or class)** led by a lead or master catechist	Regular daily religion class, plus weekly catechesis assemblies
Classroom	Classroom	**Assembly hall** with round tables for many small groups, large screens, a liturgical setting, good microphones, and a place for food to be shared.	
Students		**Participants** (or some other suitable term) Can they be called **disciples** or **apprentices in the faith?**	
Confirmation	Graduation	**Lifelong process of growing in faith**	
Volunteer classroom catechists (sometimes religion teachers)	Religion teachers	**Lead or master catechists**, table catechists for each group within the catechesis assembly, plus the essential work of each household.	
Textbook, plus other materials		**Textbook** designed for use in **Whole Community Catechesis**, plus other materials, especially (1) making use of high quality video and television programming, (2) connecting to others within the church such as missionary movements and (3) integrating family life and catechesis.	
Method—mainly to cover material in text, following instructions in teachers' or catechists' editions.		**Method**—material in text provides jumping off point for lead or master catechist to develop topic; much more serendipitous; involves households and Sunday assembly each week; generous attention is paid to everyday life; table catechists for each small group help sort all this out.	

Parents	Parents, guardians, families, or households —used interchangeably.
Mainly the work of catechesis is done by parish or school staff and volunteers; what happens is not seen as part of the process of catechesis.	**Every household** in the parish participates on a 50-50 basis; therefore, Christian home-making is part and parcel of the catechetical enterprise.
Sunday assembly is separated from catechesis.	**Weeklong reflection** (or mystagogia) on the previous Sunday's readings in every parish group and household is the basis of everything else. The homily becomes the backbone and the Eucharist is the font of all catechesis.
Sacramental prep, training for liturgical ministries, parish leader training, and preparation for pastoral care ministries are separated from catechesis programs; even the RCIA is often separated.	**Catechesis assemblies** are shaped to cover all these needs, and open to a wider range of participants as part of lifelong learning for all.
Baptism is seen as "one of the seven sacraments" and is taught as a routine part of the curriculum.	**The status of baptism** is raised to be on a par with Eucharist; catechesis on baptism and Eucharist is the backbone of all else.

Appendix 7
Outline for
Catechesis Assemblies

Here are the main features of the catechesis assemblies:

- The master or lead catechist "presides" or leads.

- Other staff for this assembly: (1) someone to coordinate hospitality (food and beverages), (2) someone to run electronic equipment, (3) one or two ministers of hospitality to help welcome folks, distribute or collect items, or perform other service duties, (4) folks to help with prayer and music, (5) folks to help take down and clean up.

- Any guests or newcomers are introduced.

- Open with prayer; music really works well. Sing songs that everyone knows and can sing with full throat.

- Begin with mystagogia on the mysteries of life and faith. This is a vital first step: read the Gospel from last Sunday's assembly and pose the Question of the Week centering on "what happened in your life this week?" Allow time for sharing at the tables.

- Use humor as much as possible—but always respectful humor, as an example for others. Humor helps folks be at ease, and it helps them see the genuine joy that comes from being near to Christ.

- Mix the ages of the participants in the room. For example, if your assembly is focused mainly on the Bible, fifth and sixth graders would find it helpful, but so would many adults. They can learn from each other. Mix them together and use the same text for them all!

- Use a method that passes the work back and forth from the lead catechist to a designated table catechist. For example, the lead catechist could begin by drawing a map of the Holy Land and helping folks become familiar with it. A short video on the modern

Middle East could be shown. Then pass the baton back to the tables and ask the learners of all ages what stories they may have heard about this part of the world. Bring some of those stories back to the large group briefly, and then move on to provide some details about the Bible. And so forth. The feeling of the assembly should be dynamic and flowing.

- Use multi-media carefully; video tends to shut down a group's participation, but there is a place for it. If used properly, it can stimulate a group as well.

- Power Point can also be useful in this setting. By preparing a presentation in outline form on Power Point, for example, a lead catechist can set the stage for the table catechists to share about their own faith.

- Keep the session moving. Think of each assembly period as a whole, and provide an interesting and lively session. The competition for this time slot is television, the internet, or a shopping mall! In order to make the faith come alive, we have to demonstrate that it is alive.

- Always have good food for the break; volunteer cooks and bakers can be recruited for this. Don't underestimate the value of a food break in a two-hour session.

- Surprise folks by changing the format. It's best for these assemblies to gather often because people get to know one another better. But vary the format from week to week. Use all the options available!

- Cover the main points in the text. The bishops of the church rightly expect us to provide everyone with a comprehensive treatment of the fundamentals of our faith.

Appendix 8
Reading List

———. *Catechism of the Catholic Church*. Collegeville, MN: The Liturgical Press, 1994.

Congregation for the Clergy. *General Directory for Catechesis*. Washington, DC: United States Catholic Conference of Bishops. 1997.

Darcy-Berube, Françoise. *Religious Education at a Crossroads*. Mahwah, NJ: Paulist Press, 1995.

Ellair, Steven. "Toward Shaping Intentional Intergenerational Communities." NCEA Catechetical Scholars Project. July 2000.

Groome, Thomas. "Spirituality as Purpose and Process of Catechesis." *The Echo Within*. Allen, TX: Thomas More, 1997.

Harris, Maria and Gabriel Moran. *Reshaping Religious Education*. Louisville, KY: Westminster/John Knox Press, 1998.

Harris, Maria. *Fashion Me a People: Curriculum in the Church*. Louisville, KY: Westminister/John Knox Press, 1989.

Huebsch, Bill. *The General Directory for Catechesis: in Plain English*. Mystic, CT: Twenty-Third Publications 2001.

Huebsch, Bill. *Vatican II in Plain English*. Allen, TX: Thomas More, 1997.

Hurley, John. "Evangelization and the Catechist." *Evangelizing Catechesis*. Washington, DC: National Conference of Catechetical Leaders (NCCL), 2000.

LaVerdiere, Eugene. *Dining in the Kingdom of God*. Chicago: Liturgy Training Publications, 1970.

Mahony, Cardinal Roger. *Guide for Sunday Mass: Gather Faithfully Together*. Chicago: Liturgy Training Publications, 1997.

————. *New Revised Standard Version Bible.* Division of Christian Education of the National Council of the Churches of Christ in the U.S.A., 1989.

————. *On Good Soil: A Tool for Parish Catechetical Renewal.* Woodland Hills, CA: Benziger, 2001.

Regan, Jane. *Toward an Adult Church.* Chicago: Loyola Press, 2002.

Roberto, John. *Generations of Faith.* Naugatuck, CT: Center for Ministry Development.

Schippe, Cullen. *The Catechist's Companion: Planting, Watering, Growing.* Woodland Hills, CA: Benziger, 1990.

Schrempf, Jeanne. "The Person of the Catechist." *Evangelizing Catechesis.* Washington, DC: NCCL, 2000.

Westerhoff, John. *Will Our Children Have Faith?* New York: Seabury, 1997.

Also by Bill Huebsch

Handbook for Success in Whole Community Catechesis

Bill Huebsch lays out the principles of whole community catechesis, offers practical steps that focus first on conversion and then on catechesis, develops suggestions and ideas for fostering households of faith, and presents several models of how whole community catechesis can work in a parish—all written in simple to understand language and a sense line format. Contains extensive reproducible pages for use in the parish, home, or school.   953083, $19.95

The General Directory for Catechesis in Plain English
A Summary and Commentary

Provides an outstanding paraphrase of the Directory with a brief study guide in the front to help readers ask thoughtful questions and focus on key points as they study the text.   951331, $10.95

People of God at Prayer
18 Services in the Spirit of Vatican II

These beautifully written prayer services, based on the major themes of Vatican II, celebrate a universal call to holiness and focus on the powerful work of the Spirit in the Church.   950122, $12.95

A New Look at Grace
A Spirituality of Wholeness

Bill Huebsch's distinctive prose images and storytelling create an unforgettable journey to the mystery and wonder of the "other side" of our everyday experiences. Here we discover anew the power and beauty of God's grace.

223558, $12.95

Heritage of Faith
A Framework for Whole Community Catechesis
Jo Rotunno

Jo Rotunno suggests that for parish-wide catechesis to be effective, a structured scope and sequence of content be incorporated into programs for parish members of all ages. She provides seven sample seasonal/doctrinal themes that are connected to the lectionary, and Questions of the Week for every week of all three years of the liturgical cycle, to foster the sharing of the Word that is at the heart of whole community catechesis.   953091, $12.95

TWENTY-THIRD PUBLICATIONS
185 WILLOW STREET • PO BOX 180 • MYSTIC, CT 06355
TEL: 1-800-321-0411 • FAX: 1-800-572-0788
Bayard   E-MAIL: ttpubs@aol.com • www.twentythirdpublications.com